IN EXTREMITY
A study of Gerard Manley Hopkins

IN EXTREMITY

A study of Gerard Manley Hopkins

JOHN ROBINSON

CAMBRIDGE UNIVERSITY PRESS

CAMBRIDGE

LONDON · NEW YORK · MELBOURNE

Published by the Syndics of the Cambridge University Press
The Pitt Building, Trumpington Street, Cambridge CB2 1RP
Bentley House, 200 Euston Road, London NW1 2DB
32 East 57th Street, New York, NY 10022, USA
296 Beaconsfield Parade, Middle Park, Melbourne 3206, Australia

First published 1978

Printed in Great Britain by W & J Mackay Limited, Chatham

Library of Congress Cataloguing in Publication Data
Robinson, John, 1943–
In extremity.
Includes index
1. Hopkins, Gerard Manley, 1844–1889 – Criticism and interpretation. I. Title.
PR4803.H44Z795   821'.8   77-77725
ISBN 0 521 21690 7

To the memory of my father

For you have but mistook me all this while:
I live with bread like you, feel want,
Taste grief, need friends

Richard II

CONTENTS

PREFACE

Gerard Hopkins led most of his daily adult life according to the instructions of a religious society, and this choice has seemed to many remarkable because he possessed outstanding creative talents and a mind conspicuously independent. Such a subordination of such an individuality they have found tragic, and they have seen the tragedy unfolding itself in his poetry: he made a disastrous mistake. Hopkins himself never said so. Wretched though he may have been at times in his calling, he does not seem ever to have doubted the rightness of his decision to join the Jesuits. Those who deplore his decision are thus upholding values different from the ones that mattered most to him.

In flat disagreement with this school are those – chiefly Catholic – who hold that it was the training he received as a Jesuit which made his poetry what it is: the Society of Jesus transformed him. The wretchedness he endured in the last years of his life is accommodated to this view only with great difficulty as an experience that is religious, though it is persistent enough and anguished enough to be an embarrassment to this cause.

This debate about whether the Jesuits were responsible for making Hopkins or for maiming him (neither seems to me to have been the case) is one which disregards the impulse of the man's own zeal and the directing power of contemporary values. While Hopkins was still a boy, Arthur Hugh Clough (in the prose Epilogue to *Dipsychus*) recognised in himself and amongst his contemporaries what he called an 'over-excitation of the religious sense', showing in an 'irrational, almost animal irritability of conscience'. Hopkins had such a sensitivity in an age propitious to its development, and thus in his intensity and his involvement with will and duty and exertion he is *of* his time; in the character of his idealism he is a representative figure.

But his interest for us is that his challenging tenacity and singleness is carried through into the excited urgency of his poetry, felt – on first acquaintance – as a pressure for attention before it is discovered as a concentration of meaning. Wordsworthian 'wise passiveness' is obviously not a major Hopkinsian potential, so much is he occupied with 'doing'. His is a poetry of conclusions or of active engagement to reach them, not of a mood of receptiveness that supposes the will to be in abeyance or the mind to be widely ranging. It is mistaken, however, to suppose that in what is generally the dense texture and energetic presence of his poetry there is not usually, waiting in the words, equivalent power of thought – though the richness of imagination in a mind and art so consciously concerned with discipline and power is something we have to discern for ourselves.

So completely was Hopkins involved with his purposes that he gives the appearance of leaving himself no still centre from which he might protect himself against the vicissitudes of experience, no detached and quiet inwardness. It is to this so-complete involvement that we should attribute, in their acuteness, the desperateness of some moments in Ireland where he is asking questions about the deepest well-springs of his being. It is this cause, too, that is responsible for Hopkins' anguish about his own creative resources, for he was constricted not by religious bonds or by narrow experience of life but by his own choking aspiration to excellence.

It is an inescapable fact that in him that aspiration found Christian form, and this is a problematic issue in considering his poetry. However, I do not think the problems are insuperable, for it seems to me that, if a religious belief is to work successfully in poetry, it must undergo the same sort of transmutation as other material; it must become part of the fabric of the poetic world and not a mere condition of entry. (As far as the poetry is concerned, for believer and sceptic alike, the relevant questions are – in the fullness of the word – ones of *sensibility*.) Sometimes Hopkins achieves this, brilliantly; sometimes he does not, and where I have written of him adversely a reader might mistakenly suppose that it is the man's faith rather than the quality of his work which stands in the way of praise. Perhaps a denial at this point will do duty for the whole book. Beliefs may be held in a multitude of ways, with differing qualities of feeling and intelligence, and such discriminations, although they will doubtless be contested in particular places, I have sought to make in discussing Hopkins' poetry.

Hopkins' virtues were those which, at the close of his preface to *Culture and Anarchy*, Arnold found to praise in the legacy of the Puritans: 'To walk staunchly by the best light one has, to be strict and sincere with oneself, not to be of the number of those who say and do not.' In pursuit of them he took the whole of his life to extremity, and the consequences are evident in his poetry, in joy and in anguish. Had he been less exacting, less intense, less determined, his poems would have been wholly different; and in this one may contrast him with Clough, in whose verse urbane, slight, smiling irony is a way of keeping possibilities open, of allowing that, while one alternative is wrong, a too fervent involvement with another may be equally mistaken: in contradistinction, Gerard Hopkins was totally committed.

ACKNOWLEDGEMENTS

To Michael Black of the Cambridge University Press and to Roger Poole for helpful comments on an early draft of this book; to Barry Done for reading the proofs and for his great, sustaining love of English; to Witold Kawalec whose friendship and whose admiration for Hopkins are recorded on the cover here; to Judy for the sympathy of many shared poems in the years-long time of this book's making.

Quotations from Hopkins' poetry and prose are made by permission of the publishers, Oxford University Press, by arrangement with the Society of Jesus (see list of sources on p. 159), and I am also grateful to the Society for permission to quote from unpublished entries in Hopkins' early diaries. A part of Ted Hughes' *Lupercal* poem 'Thrushes' appears here by permission of the publishers, Faber & Faber and Harper & Row.

1

All surrenders

On this day by God's grace I resolved to give up all beauty
until I had his leave for it.[1]

It is scarcely to be wondered at that an age schooled by Freud and
addicted to Rousseau should mistrust the Victorians: 'fulfilment' has
replaced 'self-denial' as the current shibboleth, and that in such
narrow versions that 'self-denial' has become tainted and suspect.
Some of the suspicion has attached itself to Hopkins. He burned his
early work in a gesture that 'fulfilment' has found incomprehensible,
and the flames have subsequently been seen flickering in his later
poetry,[2] and even shooting from Hell Mouth itself.[3] Against these
notions my purpose here is to argue that Hopkins' verse is at one
with his religious commitment, is attendant on the same aspirations
in the man. (I think it will be seen that this is by no means the
same as saying that it was his religious training which produced his
poetry.)

The character of Hopkins' early religious interest is ambivalent.
One impulse in it is otherworldly, retiring, serene; the other is harsh,
gruelling, energetic. The one is monastic, the other is military. In the
year after he left Oxford he made a choice between the two which,
since it serves to point up the distinctness of the two impulses as they
occur in his early poetry (for both involve discipline), is worth
recalling. By 7 May 1868 he had 'decided to be a priest and religious',
but he was 'still doubtful between St. Benedict and St. Ignatius'.[4]
He had spent the Easter of 1867 at the Benedictine Priory at Hereford, and now, after a retreat at the Jesuit house at Roehampton, he
resolved to join a religious order, and soon afterwards determined

that it should be the Society of Jesus. He had found the Hereford Priory 'a delightful place in every way';[5] in contrast, in a letter to Newman, he called the Jesuit discipline 'hard'.[6] To choose rigour thus instead of delight was entirely characteristic of Hopkins, but the consequences on this occasion were to reach through a lifetime.

The finest of his university poems are about the cloistered, not the combative, life. They are 'Heaven-Haven: A nun takes the veil' and 'The Habit of Perfection'. Both are attempts to supplant life with ritual, to make a religious ceremony (entry into an order) extend to cover all time. 'I have desired to go', says the nun of 'Heaven-Haven', and the implication of the juxtaposition in the poem's full title is instantaneous arrival, life arrested in a holy moment when there are no storms and all is 'out of the swing' of that sea whose turbulence and power Hopkins was to use more than once as a symbol of the capriciousness of time. It is not simply heaven the nun is intent on, it is sanctuary as well.

The mind at work in 'The Habit of Perfection' (once subtitled 'The Novice') is equally in search of sanctuary, and the poem equally illustrates how strong the monastic pull was to Hopkins at this time. The poem is not about renunciation but about a reallocation of sympathies which amounts to the same sort of passiveness as we have in 'Heaven-Haven'. In that poem any conscious stirrings in the nun are placed in the past, giving us the sense that they are now satisfied. In 'The Habit of Perfection' it is similarly inaction, not rejection, which is enjoined on the novice. We are taken towards exactly the kind of stasis we have in the other piece: perfection is 'still', without event, and in the first three stanzas the inclination is towards an inner life to which the exterior world of happenings is a distraction:

> Elected Silence, sing to me
> And beat upon my whorlèd ear,
> Pipe me to pastures still and be
> The music that I care to hear.
>
> Shape nothing, lips; be lovely-dumb:
> It is the shut, the curfew sent
> From there where all surrenders come
> Which only makes you eloquent.

Be shellèd, eyes, with double dark
And find the uncreated light:
This ruck and reel which you remark
Coils, keeps, and teases simple sight.

The novice is acting on – sung to, 'beat upon', sent to: the changes are all outside the 'me' who wishes them. There is no sense of a powerfully operating will (the choice of silence, for example, has already been determined before the poem begins), nor of the tension which might be involved in choice. The eyes merely 'remark' – no 'giddy judgement' here – and there is no sense of competing claims on the other two organs.

The next three stanzas might seem to threaten this poise. The words 'Palate, the hutch of tasty lust' are very obviously sensuously felt on the tongue in utterance, but how austere are not only the 'can' and 'crust' of abstinence but also the 'rinsing' for which they substitute. So remote, indeed, from imaginative realisation is any alternative to the religious life offered now in ritualised form that, by the time we come to 'O feet / That want the yield of plushy sward', it is difficult to read 'want' in the way the sense demands (that is, as 'desire'). Austerity has been so securely entered into (and 'feel-of-primrose hands' can hardly be invested with imputations of grossness or sensuality) that the feet seem to lack rather than desire the grass (grass which draws in the softness of 'plushy' only to repel in the blades of 'sward'). The continuing impression is of a controlling direction so delicately realised as to be scarcely perceptible, and consisting, finally, in the formality which takes us in logical progress through the five senses. The feast of the final stanza is wholly a matter of ritual significance: there is nothing festive about a poem whose tone is better given by the 'fasts' of an earlier stanza. The last lines (which again show the absence of effort which characterises this piece) point to the 'habit', the religious robe, of the title; but the reader is likely to feel, as in 'Heaven-Haven', that the ceremony is no initiation but, rather, a formalised moment in a life which is indeed a matter of long experience.

The felt need for repose in the two poems discussed above is to be found also in a fragment from 1866, 'The earth and heaven, so little known'. It is one of Hopkins' most interesting early pieces, for it records gracefully and without strain that wish for the dissolution of his very being which is implicit in, for example, 'No worst, there is none' and 'I wake and feel the fell of dark' (1885). The poet is confined by his own consciousness, and is, uniquely, the fixed centre of a changing world:

> The earth and heaven, so little known,
> Are measured outwards from my breast.
> I am the midst of every zone
> And justify the East and West;
>
> The unchanging register of change
> My all-accepting fixèd eye,
> While all things else may stir and range
> All else may whirl or dive or fly.

The poet is fixed in what he describes in a subsequent stanza as 'the solid world'; and in the course of the poem we have him looking enviously at the movements of a swallow, which is outside – so he fancies – the limits imposed by weight and pain. Then it becomes clear in the last three stanzas that what Hopkins has envied is not the bird's physical freedom but a sort of absence of identity which its movement between sky and earth seems to express:

> There is a vapour stands in the wind;
> It shapes itself in taper skeins:
> You look again and cannot find,
> Save in the body of the rains.
>
> And these are spent and ended quite;
> The sky is blue, and the winds pull
> Their clouds with breathing edges white
> Beyond the world; the streams are full
>
> And millbrook-slips with pretty pace
> Gallop along the meadow grass.–
> O lovely ease in change of place!
> I have desired, desired to pass...

Vapour becomes cloud, cloud rain, and the vapour loses itself; it is stream water rushing through meadows, in constant motion, in perpetual flux. The poet wishes to be part of that flux, but chiefly because this constant change will take him with the clouds, 'Beyond the world'. He has 'desired, desired to pass...' (the ellipsis is Hopkins'), and this otherworldly impulse is indistinguishable from the 'I have desired to go' theme of 'Heaven-Haven' in its wish for repose.

But Hopkins did not take that way. The young man at Oxford whom his father saw as having 'a growing love for asceticism and high ritual'[7] chose instead to go along a path which, in a sense, the age had laid down for him. The pervasive notion that spiritual excellence was arduous may have had narrowly religious origins but its power was scarcely to be accounted for by the doctrine of sect or faction. Labour, rigour, duty, seemed as virtues to have command of all the vital forces. So Tennyson felt in the 1842 Choric Song from 'The Lotus Eaters' (a song which is one of the central poems of the Victorian period, touching for that age the same spinal nerve which Shakespeare touched for all ages in 'To be or not to be'), where he was oppressed by the same analysis. He identified the life-force with strenuousness, toil, and physical difficulty (wisdom and sensitivity he could not separate from an ineffectual ennui). Thus when Hopkins chose the Jesuits he was in accord with the – in this – representative Tennysonian view that what seemed the harder course must, by virtue of its hardness, be the more virtuous.

This view is to be seen in 'New Readings' where Christ brings food from 'wastes of rock' and his way is attractive just because it is a hard way; he

> would not have that legion of winged things
> Bear Him to heaven on easeful wings.

It is present too, less obviously, in 'A Soliloquy of One of the Spies left in the Wilderness', one of Hopkins' few experiments with irony. The spy's complaints about the harsh life he is subjected to in the desert, through whose unbearable heat and barrenness Moses leads the Israelites, are set in the context of implicit Biblical reproof. The spy is not simply timorous before the trials that await him in Canaan; he is fonder of soft bondage in the irrigated gardens of Egyptian Goshen than he is of bleak duty in the sands. He sickens, and it is in the nature of his illness that he does not understand its origin, that he himself is its first cause. He has the plague – with Biblical fore-knowledge we could offer that explanation for his ailing – but he has it because he has failed his God. It is thus alienation from Yahweh which is expressed in his mysterious sickness. There is perhaps something suggestive about the fact that the spy gathers the lotus (here the flower, not the fruit of the tree); at any rate his fate, even in the poem, is languid and ineluctable.

According to some translations Paul the apostle hurt his body and made it know its master;[8] so (from 'Easter Communion' with its 'You striped in secret with breath-taking whips') did the religious circles in which Hopkins moved; so also, if we trust his biographical warranty for 'The Wreck of the Deutschland' with its 'lashed rod' ('what refers to myself in the poem is all strictly and literally true and did all occur'[9]), did Hopkins himself. Penances, denials, chastenings – the harshness of the Lent spirit with its conviction that if something is enjoyed there is spiritual value or benefit in giving it up – are much in evidence in early Hopkins. They do not amount to real asceticism (they are periodic, and in their nature suppose some ordinarily more indulgent style of life) and may, perhaps for that reason, produce sensuous experiences which are questionable. Pleasure is quickened by denial which may become, because of this, part of the experience of pleasure: this is one mood in the early Hopkins, for example in 'Easter Communion', where every abnegation issues into some compensatory richness, a feature repeated in 'Easter' with its 'Beauty now for ashes wear, / Perfumes for the garb of woe'. The very intensity of religious ardour may be disquieting to someone who does not share it; when that ardour seems to involve some affection for physical suffering this problem of sympathy becomes extreme: at times in the early work the attraction the hard life had for Hopkins topples over into masochism.

We meet it in Hopkins' schoolboy poem 'The Escorial'. Throughout his life Hopkins had a regard for those who had been put to death for their faith. In 1864 he wrote 'For a Picture of St. Dorothea' (Dorothea was martyred *c*. 303), later he wrote on another martyr, 'St. Thecla', and, in 1875–6, he bestowed a sort of martyrdom on the five nuns in 'The Wreck of the Deutschland' (whose death at the behest of 'Thou martyr-master' is an indirect consequence of religious intolerance). From his time in Wales we have a short piece on St Winefred, beheaded in flight, restored to life by St Beuno, and the cause of the spring at Holywell (later her story was the plot of an unfinished play), and subsequently he began a poem on

Margaret Clitheroe who was pressed to death in York in 1586 for sheltering Catholic priests. He projected an ode on Edmund Campion to be finished for 1 December 1881, the three-hundredth anniversary of his martyrdom – though this he never managed. In 'The Escorial' Hopkins writes, in part, about St Lawrence, the martyr whose death is remembered by the erection of the building.

Hopkins has been criticised for his treatment of the subject. Elizabeth Schneider sees the poem as 'marked by an inclination to dwell upon physical torture, cruelty, and martyrdom',[10] and comments, 'Already...there were signs of emotion deflected into unusual and, to many readers perhaps, somewhat repellent channels.'[11] The description of the martyrdom is indeed horrible (chiefly because of the second line here):

> For that staunch saint still prais'd his Master's name
> While his crack'd flesh lay hissing on the grate;
> Then fail'd the tongue; the poor collapsing frame,
> Hung like a wreck that flames not billows beat –

and one's instinctive defence – that these, after all, are lines by a fifteen-year-old in whom mature balance might not be reasonably expected yet – must be set aside in the light of some of Hopkins' Oxford poems. When he was nineteen he produced the uncompleted 'Pilate', where Christ's judge plans his own crucifixion, trying mentally to resolve the technical problems of killing himself – and this in details which serve, it would seem, no larger purpose:

> I'll take in hand the blady stone
> And to my palm the point apply,
> And press it down, on either side a bone,
> With hope, with shut eyes, fixedly;
> Thus crucified as I did crucify.

This is morbid; but Miss Schneider's 'Already...there were signs' implies that this morbid element in Hopkins became more pronounced. In fact it is less and less evident in his work. The development in his poetry is away from this element, not towards it.

He had at the outset, we may be sure, a view of suffering which is odd to someone not sharing his religious convictions – and perhaps unsatisfyingly simple to someone who does (a view which we shall meet again in 'The Wreck of the Deutschland') – but one at least

logically consistent with the faith of one who believed that God is
'throned behind / Death with a sovereignty that heeds but hides.'
('The Wreck of the Deutschland', stanza 32). It showed characteristically when Robert Bridges' brother-in-law and young baby had
been brutally murdered and Bridges' sister (Mrs Plow), herself
wounded in the same attack, died of grief a year later.[12] Hopkins
wrote in sympathy (it is the last sentence of the quotation which is
significant; I give the earlier ones to set the context fairly):

My dear Bridges, – It is nearly a fortnight since my mother gave me the sad
news of Mrs. Plow's death but I have not till today had an opportunity of writing
to you, as I wished to do. I cannot help thinking that perhaps for her own sake
she could not have much wished to live longer with such dreadful grief upon her
memory...No doubt her health never really recovered the first shock. What
suffering she had! Even during Mr. Plow's life she had troubles, you told me,
and it appeared in her face. But sufferings falling on such a person as your sister
was are to be looked on as the marks of God's particular love and this is truer the
more exceptional they are.[13]

The confident proposition that inflicted suffering is a sign of love is
difficult to take.

Hopkins turned aside from that monasticism which might have
given him serenity, choosing instead a discipline that was military in
character and in which, in the event, the elements of change and toil
were ones to which he was to prove temperamentally and physically
unsuited. The tension thus caused between his ideal of holiness and
what might have suited his more mundane needs is at the root of
much of his Irish poetry. As such it is the subject of a later chapter,
but the point to be made here is that the character of his poetry was
essentially the character of his life. When the poet who, throughout
his life, greatly valued the 'astonishing'[14] genius of Keats recon-
sidered his estimate, seeing besides the genius 'unmanly and
enervating luxury', he was marking out his own development – that
of the 'austerer utterance in art'[15] that he believed Keats would have
achieved had he lived longer. Very early in his life Hopkins had left
behind the cloying richness of 'The Escorial' and 'A Vision of the
Mermaids' and transmuted it into something more serviceable. It
is in complete accord with the view of Hopkins I have given so far
that he should find luxury 'enervating'. 'Masculine' (in opposition to
the unmanliness of much Keats) is the word Hopkins reaches for

whenever he particularly wishes to praise a poet he admires. Art – the art on which he appeared to turn his back when he burned his poetry – derived its being, as Pater and his followers saw it, from sensation not action; it shared in the passivity of the lotus eaters, the death-lapse, the poppy. In a sense, then, it was not his own poetry that drove him to turn his verses to ashes so much as other people's: even after he had started writing again he observed to Bridges in 1877, 'It seems that triolets and rondels and rondeaus and chants royal and what not and anything but serving God are all the fashion.'[16]

It was the will, not the appetite, Hopkins sought to bring into submission. His many resounding resolutions to do with 'giving up' were, in fact, all provisional – temporary expedients for showing himself where his heart lay. He abandoned them in time. With this in view I turn to the history of his decision to destroy his early work, a decision which seems more than any other of his to challenge the idea of the unity of his spiritual energy.

Hopkins told Canon Dixon (formerly a master at the school he attended as a boy) that he had burned his poetry before becoming a Jesuit and, for seven years, 'wrote nothing but two or three little presentation pieces which occasion called for'.[17] At the end of this period he produced 'The Wreck of the Deutschland'. The apparent contradiction between this sudden-seeming achievement and the destruction which preceded it seven years earlier has given to Hopkins' life an unwarranted ambiguity. He has been seen as a Jekyll and Hyde:[18] guilty priest, thwarted poet. The truth is very different, and it is worth pointing out even at this stage in the discussion that the details – the small print beneath Hopkins' headline account – belie the notion of some frantic attempt, in the fashion of Aubrey Beardsley's, to obliterate the past. Hopkins' friends retained their copies of his poems, and he made no attempt to erase the ones to be found in his diaries. (Incidentally, amongst the cancelled confession-notes which have been omitted from the published version of these diaries[19] are ones referring to 'scrupulosity'[20] and 'scrupulosity abt poems'.[21])

We should take Hopkins' burning of his poems as a renunciation of all hopes of that public world in which he might expect an audience – the art-world of Swinburne, Pater, and the rondeliers. It marked a reorientation in his life which was, in the event, an affirmation of his own independence, for to say, as Hopkins did in 1878, that 'The only just judge, the only just literary critic, is Christ',[22] is effectively to disregard the pressing claims of others. However, if this was the effect of the burning, it certainly was not its purpose, which was rather in the nature of a demonstration to himself of where his sympathies lay, a token.

Hopkins was inclined to fix his life by self-made resolutions, and these have – as the burning has – a note of finality which subsequent events belie. Thus he wrote to an Oxford friend in July 1867:

I had not forgotten I had promised to copy you out a thing of mine, but first I had to make some alterations which I cd not settle to my satisfaction in that preoccupied time of reading for the schools, during which I had made a rule – with a partial exception in the case of this piece – to have nothing to do with versemaking.[23]

The rule was made but almost immediately qualified. There is even more weightiness about the epigraph to this chapter (a diary entry of 6 November 1865); giving up was plainly with Hopkins a means of self-discipline, but he did not 'give up' beauty (whatever that means exactly) in any notable way for any great length of time. The heaviness of the wording – and the fact that it is now perpetuated in print – gives to the daily fluctuations of a scrupulous conscience an unjustified rigidity. Hopkins outgrew his own restrictions.

This is obvious in the case of Welsh. His Journal entry for 6 September 1874 (shortly after going to Wales for training) has this in it:

Indeed in coming here I began to feel a desire to do something for the conversion of Wales. I began to learn Welsh too but not with very pure intentions perhaps. However on consulting the Rector on this, the first day of the retreat, he discouraged it unless it were purely for the sake of labouring among the Welsh. Now it was not and so I saw I must give it up...I had no sooner given up the Welsh than my desire seemed to be for the conversion of Wales and I had it in mind to give up everything else for that; nevertheless weighing this by St. Ignatius' rules of election I decided not to do so.[24]

There is a deal of 'giving up' here and the sinuous way desire suits itself to conscience is something to smile over, but the passage tells only part of the story: Hopkins went on to become reasonably competent in Welsh and there is no further expression of qualms on the subject. The casual reader risks making more of this entry than Hopkins did himself.

Burning poems was obviously more important for Hopkins than deciding whether or not to learn Welsh, but the same is true of that too. It was a token, and Professor MacKenzie seems to me to give its significance exactly when he says, 'he resolved to burn his poems as a symbolic act, very much as St Francis of Assisi stripped himself of his worldly clothes at the start of his new life'.[25] It was not Hopkins' commitment to the priesthood but the even more rigorous dedication to a religious order which prompted his abandonment of verse – a fact which needs to be distinguished. Contrast Hopkins' letter to Baillie of February 1868 –

I want to write still and as a priest I very likely can do that too, not so freely as I shd. have liked, e.g. nothing or little in the verse way, but no doubt what wd. best serve the cause of my religion[26]

– with the severity of the utterances which came after his May resolution, when he felt that his poems 'wd. interfere with my state and vocation'[27] and he 'resolved to write no more'.[28] That the burning was symbolic rather than practical is further supported by the way he writes to Bridges in 1868, a little more than two months after the probable date (11 May) on which he burned his poems.[29] He says, 'I kept however corrected copies of some things which you have and will send them'[30] – the gesture (the burning) has been made; however, this is not allowed to interfere with artistic pride, with the scrupulously careful last touch. Similarly, the token burning does not stop Hopkins from hoping to raise money for a holiday in Switzerland by writing an article on William Morris and 'the medieval school of poets'. This, he says, will be his swan song – if it ever gets written.[31]

Until he wrote 'To R. B.' (1889), in which he speaks of 'hand at work now never wrong', his stated attitude to poetry remained constant: verse-making was not one of the duties of a religious and, since the duties of a religious should occupy most of his life, there could be only a small place for poetry – it was something to be fitted in as time allowed. When his duties altered and gave him more free time he was depressed by the little he could produce, but not until his priestly life became completely unsatisfying (later on in Ireland) did 'poetry and production'[32] become the main aspirations in his daily life. Thus, in 1877, he scruples about writing a letter on rhythm (he was to write many) because it is an 'unprofessional matter'.[33] By contrast, in 1882, the commentary he is writing on Ignatius' *Spiritual Exercises* is 'very professional'.[34] Indeed the question of professionalism is recurrent in his letters. He tells Dixon that for seven years he wrote nothing 'as not belonging to my profession',[35] and it is this sense we should bear in mind when Hopkins writes in 1884, while still relatively new to Ireland, that 'it always seems to me that poetry is unprofessional'.[36] His single-mindedness shows again when, in 1881, he worries to Dixon about 'the waste of time the very compositions you admire may have caused and their preoccupation of the mind which belonged to more sacred or more binding duties'.[37] (Note the way 'more binding' is immediately offered in exchange for 'more sacred'.) Thus, when Patmore does what Hopkins himself did years before and burns some of his work, the Jesuit's comment is that 'When we take a step like this we are forced to condemn ourselves: either our work shd. never have been done or never undone, and either way our time and our toil are wasted.'[38] This is Hopkins' mature judgement on his own action. When it is taken in conjunction with his belief that 'my vocation puts before me a standard so high that a higher can be found nowhere else'[39] Hopkins' destruction of his early work falls into true perspective.

Unfortunately this view is easily confused with another which supposes that dark and subconscious forces were at work in Hopkins' choice; and to misunderstand Hopkins' burning of his poems is to begin to misunderstand his later life. Conversely, if that decision is properly understood, one will tend to resist views such as the one Father Devlin proposes on this (he is here discussing Hopkins' appointment to teach Classics at Stonyhurst College in September 1882):

Confronted with the perfect neatness of the Provincial's mind, with his massive and smoothly-moving deliberation, a wave of diffidence amounting almost to despair seeped up in Hopkins. It was borne in upon him that he must look on his poetic genius as an amiable weakness which a hard-working Jesuit might indulge for an hour or two occasionally. And he grasped, half-consciously but once and for all, that the secret 'wildness' of his inspiration could never be channelled in that manner.[40]

Hopkins' mind had been made up long before this; and his inspiration was never 'wildness' (it was 'enthusiasm',[41] 'rapture'[42] even, but never marked by the lawlessness and indiscipline which 'wildness' connotes), nor was it 'secret' if secret be supposed to have connotations of furtiveness. Furthermore, there is nothing in the relevant September letter to suggest that Hopkins was obliged to see his interest in poetry as a weakness. (Within a fortnight he had finished and was pleased with 'The Leaden Echo and the Golden Echo', begun the previous year.)

It would be mistaken, then, to suggest that the Society of Jesus as such suppressed his creative impulse. 'I am always jaded, I cannot tell why, and my vein shews no signs of ever flowing again', [43] Hopkins wrote while still based at Stonyhurst in March of the following year; and this is hardly the language of somebody who feels he should not be doing what he is so obviously failing to do anyway.

It is Father Devlin's use of the phrase 'half-consciously' which is particularly misleading because it introduces the possibility of fierce inner tensions of which the poet himself was scarcely aware (a possibility which, I hope to show later, has caused the meanings of some of his poems – notably of 'The Windhover' – to be severely distorted by some of Hopkins' readers). Thus Father Devlin can subsequently say of Hopkins' move to Ireland:

There are indications in the notes how his outraged nature (that is, his poetic genius) wreaked its revenge. It curled itself around his beloved country, 'England...wife to my creating thought', and enlisted his patriotism and sense of justice against his vow of obedience. It entangled itself demonstratively in the endless labyrinth of examination papers, emphasizing the slavery to which it was being subjected.[44]

This clearly suggests that in Ireland Hopkins was in the grip of some titanic force quite outside his control and quite beyond his understanding (whose power it had usurped). By making it appear that Hopkins was finding excuses for himself this takes the justice out of the complaints he made in his letters and, in that way, makes him culpable for the misery he was often in. How far this situation is from the truth I hope to show in my final chapter; for the present, it should be seen that this misreading derives initially from a misconception of the reasons for Hopkins' failing inspiration, a misconception which would not arise if sufficient importance were attached to his reasons for burning his verse.

Hopkins went back on his decision not to write (the flimsy ground that his superior wished someone would write a poem about the 'Deutschland' was the reason Hopkins gave for abandoning a restriction that his maturer intelligence may now have found not so much irksome as obsolete), but his attitude to poetry remained consistent. In his attitude to publication there is more fluctuation. The monastic pull, the pull of the sanctuary, is once more in evidence. He is certainly alert to the risks involved in fame that publication might bring: it 'gives them "itching ears" and makes them live on public breath',[45] he says. It is not poetry but publication (with its 'thoughts of vainglory'[46]) which constitutes the real problem for the spiritual life: 'genius attracts fame and individual fame St. Ignatius looked on as the most dangerous and dazzling of all attractions',[47] he tells Dixon. Hopkins (in 1881) will thus be entirely passive in the matter of publication, resigning himself to the possibility of continuing obscurity:

When a man has given himself to God's service, when he has denied himself and followed Christ, he has fitted himself to receive and does receive from God a special guidance, a more particular providence. This guidance is conveyed partly by the action of other men, as his appointed superiors, and partly by direct lights and inspirations. If I wait for such guidance, through whatever channel conveyed, about anything, about my poetry for instance, I do more wisely in every way than if I try to serve my own seeming interests in the matter. Now if you [Dixon] value what I write, if I do myself, much more does our Lord. And if he chooses to avail himself of what I leave at his disposal he can do so with a felicity and with a success which I could never command. And if he does not, then two things follow; one that the reward I shall nevertheless receive from him will be all the greater; the other that then I shall know how much a thing contrary to his will and even to my own best interests I should have done if I had taken things into my own hands and forced on publication. This is my principle and this in the main has been my practice.[48]

However, Hopkins' motives for not publishing were ambiguous. Publication would mean not only fame and vainglory but also exposure. This he feared throughout his life. We recall the 'cumbrous shame' which makes the Alchemist leave the city ('The Alchemist in the City'); and a year earlier (1864) Hopkins had written to Baillie about his being accustomed 'to conceal what I write except from you'[49] (a habit he certainly broke later by, for example, giving copies of poems to Urquhart[50] and Bridges[51]).

The fear of criticism or opposition extended to his work as a priest in Oxford: 'I used indeed to fear when I went up about this time last year that people wd. repeat against me what they remembered to my disadvantage.'[52] It entered into his feelings about publishing his poetry. Perhaps it shows in his instruction to his mother when there is some possibility of *The Month* accepting 'The Wreck of the Deutschland': 'You must never say that the poem is mine.'[53] Certainly it is present in his anxious order to Canon Dixon when his former schoolmaster is on the point of sending poems of his to the Carlisle newspapers (in 1879):

Pray do not send the piece to the paper: I cannot consent to, I forbid its publication. You must see that to publish my manuscript against my expressed wish is a breach of trust...what is not near enough for public fame may be more than enough for private notoriety, which is what I dread.[54]

It is not the spiritual danger of fame which is troubling Hopkins here, but the censure of his colleagues. Seven years later when Dixon dedicates a 'Bible Birthday Book' anthology of texts and poems to Hopkins, and asks that one of his stanzas should be included, the same anxiety shows in reply:

The dedication: this is a great honour, which on the one hand I do not like to decline but which nevertheless I have some dread of, for I do not want my name to be before the public. It is true your poems do not command a large public, unhappily; but then the small one might contain enemies, so to call people, of mine. So do which you think best: if you dedicate I am flattered, if you do not I am reassured.

I think there could be no objection to my lines appearing in the Birthday Book, especially anonymously (as I should wish)[55]

This extraordinary reference to 'enemies' is repeated in Hopkins' retreat-notes for 1883. Hopkins shows in the notes that he is afraid, not of any spiritual risk which his poems might entail but of the way they make him vulnerable:

Also in some med. today I earnestly asked our Lord to watch over my compositions, not to preserve them from being lost or coming to nothing, for that I am

very willing they should be, but they might not do me harm through the enmity
or imprudence of any man or my own[56]

Yet with the fear of vulnerability there is mingled in Hopkins a
deep hunger for acceptance. In 1881 Dixon had made an attempt to
get something by Hopkins published in Hall Caine's sonnet
anthology and Hopkins co-operated readily, without expressing
misgivings.[57] The wry irony of Caine's subsequent rejection of
Hopkins' work as not conforming with the complacent purpose of
the book (to 'demonstrate the impossibility of improving upon the
acknowledged structure whether as to rhyme-scheme or measure'[58])
together with his decision 'to refute me in a special paragraph'[59] may
well have been in Hopkins' mind when he gave his so-reluctant reply
to Dixon – as might Coventry Patmore's more recent and very
adverse letter of 20 March 1884.[60] Moreover, there is in his later
utterances a growing wistfulness for wider recognition: 'what I want
there, to be more intelligible, smoother, and less singular, is an
audience'.[61] 'I would have you and Canon Dixon and all true poets
remember that fame, the being known, though in itself one of the
most dangerous things to man, is nevertheless the true and appointed
air, element, and setting of genius and its works.'[62] (Ironically, it was
only three months earlier in 1886 that he had expressed reservations
to Dixon about the dedication.) Again, to Bridges he says, 'What you
say about the run of people not liking nor knowing what to make of
your writing and this giving you satisfaction opens out a wide vein
of to me saddening thoughts.'[63] Hopkins wavers, then, between
desire for recognition and fear of what the public scrutiny it involves
might bring.

As a poet Hopkins' first judge is always Christ, and only in Ireland
does he acknowledge that the absence of an audience has affected
him adversely. Before this it is scarcely conceivable that a poet could
be harsher on his potential readers. The public are 'random, reckless,
incompetent, and unjust'.[64] Their judgement is limiting, so that 'The
Blessed Virgin compared to the Air we Breathe' is 'partly a com-
promise with popular taste',[65] and 'The May Magnificat' and 'The
Silver Jubilee' are '"popular" pieces, in which I feel myself to come
short'.[66] When he fails to get the early 'Beyond the Cloister'
accepted (1867) he says to Urquhart, 'I need not alter what I cannot

publish',[67] and, ten years later, he makes an almost identical comment to Bridges about 'The Wreck of the Deutschland':

> I cannot think of altering anything. Why shd. I? I do not write for the public. You are my public and I hope to convert you.[68]

If this belligerent independence – the independence of 'Write no bilgewater about it'[69] – softened as the years passed ('one ought to be independent but not unimpressionable'[70]), Hopkins' sense that poetic talent is Christ-given and to be employed by him remained unaltered. Here in his Lord is the one who prizes 'more than any man...the gifts of his own making'.[71] Hopkins' lifelong obscurity gave him much-needed security; his commitment to the Jesuits buttressed his own poetic individuality.

There is some irony in the fact that a poet who practised austerities at Oxford and who afterwards made over the whole of his life in disciplined obedience should have been taught while at university by a man such as Walter Pater. However, the experience brings into focus important questions about Hopkins' own development; it is amongst those that I treat in my next chapter.

2

Pater, and the Falcon

A mode of seeing

...one must hold ideas loosely in the relative spirit...not
disquiet oneself about the absolute.[1]

I have so far described Hopkins pursuing an idea of moral perfection
characterised by rigour and subjugation of will. He attempted just as
determinedly to discover the ideal in the visible world, convinced
that when he had apprehended it he had in some way apprehended
with particular intimacy the presence of God in created nature. As it
shows in his poetry this search in the beautiful has opened him to
accusations (accusations more put about than published) of 'mere
aestheticism', of – much misunderstood phrase – 'art for art's sake'.
It seems to me true that there were times when his love of beauty
impeded him and spoiled his judgement, but 'aestheticism' carries
with it the suggestion that Hopkins was committed to a programme
or nexus of values which he actually opposed. This is not the place
to recover for the aesthetic movement some reputation for penetrating understanding of what had gone wrong in the inner life of the
nineteenth century (carefully read, Pater's *Appreciations* essay on
Wordsworth and Swinburne's study of Blake would do that), for
diagnostic insight alone does not exonerate that movement from
criticism. I mention that insight simply to point out that the unfair-
ness in charging Hopkins with 'mere aestheticism' is a double one.
I take Walter Pater as being sufficiently representative of aestheticism
to give to the comparison of his thought and Hopkins' which I make
in this chapter a wider significance than the merely personal. The
two were ultimately in opposition, but that opposition is better
understood as a divergence than as a confrontation. In part, then,

Pater is included here to show the continuity in Hopkins' development, the how and why of his evolution both before and after he
joined the Jesuits. However, the two men did diverge: Pater's other
role here is to present the contrast with those values which for
Hopkins came to inhere in 'the Falcon'. Pater is both mentor and foil.

I also include here considerations of Hopkins' own coinages
'inscape' and 'instress', which sometimes relate to his discovery of
the ideal, but which, though he never abandoned the concepts they
express, seem to have mattered far more to him in early manhood
than in later life: in terms of the development of his poetry the ideas
discussed in this chapter have limited application. Emotionally they
are perhaps significant as signs of a need in Hopkins to surround
himself with certitude. Since Hopkins came to his conviction by
degrees, I have risked some temporary loss of clarity by discussing
'inscape' and 'instress' in chronological sequence (i.e. after my
treatment of Pater, in which 'inscape' occurs, and not before) since
this leads most readily to the ideas of John Duns Scotus. The last
part of this chapter is concerned with Hopkins' most complex poetic
expression of his discovery of the ideal, 'The Windhover'.

Hopkins' Journal and his early diaries are full of scraps of poetry and
studied observations in prose on elements of the natural world, some
of which were to be incorporated in poems written many years later.
They seem to encourage the idea that, early or late, the same mind
is at work, with the same terms of reference. However, it should be
noted that always Hopkins is building from fragments written when
the essential synthesis was still to come.

We may notice, for example, that more than eleven years before he
was to write 'The Starlight Night' with its 'piece-bright paling' he
recorded,

> The stars were packed so close that night
> They seemed to press and stare
> And gather in like hurdles bright
> The liberties of air.[2]

Again, the idea in 'The Sea and the Skylark' (1877) that a bird
unwinds music to earth beneath is prefigured in a fragment which
fancies 'that the concording stars / Had let such music down'.[3] The

image of collapsing embers which closes 'The Windhover' was one
which Hopkins had used – with a different connotation – in 1864:

> Death's bones fell in with sudden clank
> As wrecks of minèd embers will.[4]

In 'A Soliloquy of One of the Spies left in the Wilderness' there is
the same transferred epithet ('they who crush the oil') as in 'God's
Grandeur' ('the ooze of oil / Crushed'). Professor Gardner has
shown[5] how 'Hurrahing in Harvest' and 'That Nature is a Heraclitean Fire' make use of details set down many years earlier. The same
is true for other poems. Probably unconsciously, Hopkins quarried
his own early ideas, and difficulties are sometimes resolved when the
reader refers back. In 1865 Hopkins described clouds in the way he
was later to describe Harry Ploughman's muscles: they were
'comparable to barrows, arranged of course in parallels'.[6] In 1866 he
noted 'Drops of rain hanging on rails etc. seen with only the lower
rim lighted like nails (of fingers)...Vermilion look of the hand held
against a candle with the darker parts as the middles of the fingers
and especially the knuckles covered with ash.'[7] This gave him, later,
'The moon, dwindled and thinned to the fringe of a fingernail held
to the candle' ('Moonrise', 1876). In May 1866 he noted the
'Beautiful blackness and definition of elm tree branches in evening
light (from behind)',[8] and in the following year that the elm leaves
'chip the sky',[9] and that he had seen 'isles of leaf all ricked and
beaked'[10] – experiences which are built into 'the beakleaved boughs
dragonish damask the tool-smooth bleak light' of 'Spelt from
Sibyl's Leaves'. The 'folded rank' of trees in 'Binsey Poplars' had
something in common with those in Richmond Park which were 'in
distinctly projected, crisp, and almost hard, rows of loaves, their
edges, especially at the top, being a little fixed and shaped with
shadow',[11] or with the yews along the approach to Manresa House
which appeared as 'bright flat pieces like wings in a theatre...each
shaped by its own sharp-cut shadow falling on the yew-tree next
behind it'.[12] The fellsides of the Isle of Man were 'plotted and
painted with the squares of the fields'[13] as the 'Landscape plotted
and pieced' of 'Pied Beauty' (1877), and the idea of 'The Starlight
Night' (1877) that the stars shut 'home' Christ is clearly developing
three years earlier in Devon:

As we drove home the stars came out thick: I leant back to look at them and my heart opening more than usual praised our Lord to and in whom all that beauty comes home.[14]

Even earlier still (1864) he had noted in a diary 'The fields of heaven covered with eye-brights. – White-diapered with stars',[15] which, by its comparison of the skies with the ground, anticipates 'the grey lawns cold' of the 1877 poem. Hopkins' habit (till 1875) of keeping detailed notes helped sustain him later as a poet and was indeed in itself a creative activity.

There is promise of development, too, in Hopkins' very awareness of the observing process which begins to show early in 'A Vision of the Mermaids'. He says of sunset,

> Where the eye fix'd, fled the encrimsoning spot,
> And gathering, floated where the gaze was not.

This, in itself, is of little consequence, but the awareness shown here that vision is not a simple mechanical process has become something more complex by the time he writes a fragment about a rainbow (August 1864):

> It was a hard thing to undo this knot.
> The rainbow shines, but only in the thought
> Of him that looks. Yet not in that alone,
> For who makes rainbows by invention?
> And many standing round a waterfall
> See one bow each, yet not the same to all,
> But each a hand's breadth further than the next.
> The sun on falling waters writes the text
> Which yet is in the eye or in the thought.
> It was a hard thing to undo this knot.

This piece evidences Hopkins' intense curiosity about the real nature of visible things and a recognition that perception contains an intellectual component crucial to the experience of seeing. Seeing was to become for him a way of realising the security of absolute truths in a world subject to change. It is sufficient for a moment, though, to see Hopkins trying to grasp fully what he has observed. Thus, four years later (1868), he writes in his Journal of fir and beech woods in Switzerland, 'the spraying was baffling and beautiful',[16] and, in 1871, 'The bluebells in your hand baffle you with their inscape, made to every sense.'[17] (This awareness of himself as an active agent of perception – for 'Unless you refresh the mind from time to time you cannot always remember or believe how deep the inscape in things is'[18] – was brought to its highest pitch in 'The Windhover'.)

The foregoing comments indicate considerable continuity between the way Hopkins reacted to nature in his Oxford days and the way he responded after he left. The major and crucial exception is the absence from his Oxford prose and poetry of any vital connection between his faith and his love of natural beauty. Thus far, then, the evidence points to the conclusion that the Society of Jesus was central in enabling him to make the fusion which is at the core of the poetry he wrote in Wales, and that, far from being the cause of friction between his religion and his love of natural beauty, the Society in some way linked these two major elements in him. As I understand its place in Hopkins' life, it presented no obstacle to such a link, but the intellectual possibility for such a connection is opened up in Hopkins not by the teachings of St Ignatius but by a philosophy of form which Hopkins was developing even before he left Oxford.

Others have thought differently. The claim for the central importance of Jesuit training in Hopkins' development as a poet is advanced in two ways. The first is to say (I quote from David Downes' book) that 'the methods of Ignatian meditation are very much akin to the creative processes of the imagination, and this being so, had considerable artistic influence on Hopkins' poetry'.[19] The second is to argue that 'the Ignatian discipline had transformed him', and that Hopkins' 'poetic experience originated primarily from his learning and living the *Spiritual Exercises* of St. Ignatius Loyola'.[20]

As far as the first argument is concerned, Ignatian meditation *makes use* of 'the creative processes of the imagination'; it is not *akin* to them (Ignatius speaks of seeing 'with the eye of the imagination the corporeal place where the object I wish to contemplate is found'[21]). It can thus be said to encourage the workings of the imagination but only by directing them toward a predetermined end (the process is shown in chapter 3 of James Joyce's *A Portrait of the Artist as a Young Man* where Father Arnall conducts a retreat).

With this in mind, it would be fair to claim that, for example, stanza 3 of 'The Wreck of the Deutschland' with its immediate sense of 'the hurtle of hell / Behind' seems to owe something to Ignatius' Fifth Exercise of the First Week (envisioning hell[22]). Further, Ignatius makes extensive use of the colloquy,[23] of direct address to God, and one can see Hopkins – as Donne did – employing that method, for example, in the opening stanza of 'The Wreck of the Deutschland' (though one would be hard pressed to maintain conclusively that a more general tradition of prayer would not have had a similar effect). It is at least possible that he would not have made use of the colloquy – or such distinguished use of it – if he had not been accustomed to it by retreats, though this is open to debate.

However, very little of Hopkins' poetry is about the particular concerns of the *Spiritual Exercises* insofar as they focus on specific events and places (the rebellion in heaven, Christ's crucifixion, hell, the nativity, etc.). Thus the second argument – that Hopkins' experience derives from his living the *Spiritual Exercises* – is advanced on the line that Hopkins' poems are imbued with a *spirit* which is distinctively Ignatian. (The *Spiritual Exercises* which are primarily a *method* could not be expected to provide much of the *substance* of Hopkins' poems.) Here the claim for the decisive influence of Hopkins' Jesuit training breaks down. It does so because, apart from the militarism of Ignatius, the attempted definition of the Ignatian spirit is too general. To the question 'What is meant, then, by Ignatian?' we have this reply:

Ignatius stressed a triune God of action in the Exercises: God, the Father (in the Principle and Foundation, and the First Week) Who created, punished, and disinherited man; Christ, the Son (Second, Third and Fourth Weeks) Who became man, and redeemed mankind, Who continues to send His aid to man, and asks other men to help Him in His labors; the Holy Spirit (Contemplation for obtaining Love) Who infuses into men knowledge and love of the Divine Being. Another notable aspect of the Exercises is that Christ is the central figure. For Ignatius, Christ is the supreme event in mankind's history, for through Him man's destiny is again made divine. These characteristics make up what I have called the Ignatian vision: Ignatius' world view. They represent his particular view of Christianity.[24]

However, there is nothing in this description which does not apply equally to St Paul, or to John Wesley: it does not adequately delimit. This is not a fault for which the writer is exclusively

responsible, for the problem of defining 'Ignatian' derives primarily
from the nature of the *Spiritual Exercises* themselves. They propose
a system, a technique; they do not constitute a distinctive body of
doctrine. Accordingly it is virtually impossible to decide that a
particular writer, if he is in any case Christian, has been decisively
influenced by them. The further argument for Ignatian influence,
that 'the Ignatian man uses all things in so far as they lead him back
to God',[25] depends on but a small part of the *Exercises* (Ignatius'
directions on the proper use of creatures[26]) and applies with greater
force to St Francis (whom, as patron of the drowned nuns, Hopkins
revered in stanza 23 of 'The Wreck of the Deutschland'). It is
perhaps in Ignatius' second point in his 'Contemplation for obtaining
Love' that he comes closest to some quality that one can identify as
being in Hopkins. Ignatius' instruction is 'to consider how God
dwells in the creatures; in the elements, giving them being; in the
plants, giving them growth; in the animals, giving them sensation;
in men, giving them understanding; and so in me'.[27] However, here
again the direction is too general to be decisive.

In fact it was not Ignatius' *Spiritual Exercises* but Hopkins' ideas
about form which were to prove central in his growth, and the most
important general influence on him here seems to have been the most
obvious, least surprising of all: Plato's. However, as those ideas were
formulated in relation to art their development was distinctive, and
it is here that I turn to Pater as something other than an opponent of
Hopkins' faith, not because he was the only source from which they
might have come but because he was the nearest important point of
personal interchange. There are interesting affinities, even if the
evidence for some formative effect is all of a tenuous prima facie
kind, and the differences too are instructive.

That Pater was, formally, Hopkins' mentor is a matter of historical
fact: he taught the undergraduate for a term in 1866, and thereafter
relations between the two men continued intermittently for twelve
years. When this is recalled, the explicit record is strikingly bald and
the lack of comment from Hopkins is noticeable in comparison with
his remarks on other figures who gained some public standing.
Carlyle was 'morally an imposter', 'a false prophet',[28] Matthew

Arnold 'a rare genius and a great critic',[29] Ruskin had 'the insight of a dozen critics'[30] but often went astray,[31] Newman's prose style was 'the flower of the best Oxford life' but still mistaken,[32] Dickens had no real control of pathos,[33] Gladstone – Hopkins intemperately agreed – ought to be beheaded.[34] And Pater? In 1867 Hopkins was expecting an invitation from him to spend time at Sidmouth with him but this did not arrive.[35] In 1868, when he briefly returned to Oxford, he had lunch with him.[36] It was flattering, in 1878, to hear that Pater remembered him and still took an interest in him;[37] and, when Hopkins went back to Oxford later that year to assist with a parish, 'Pater was one of the men I saw most of'.[38] But about his philosophy Hopkins' Journal simply records, 'Pater talking two hours against Xtianity';[39] there is no further comment.

Perhaps it was the huge philosophical divide between them that made Hopkins' references to Pater so spare, for Pater's antipathy to Christianity was indeed marked, and yet when Hopkins returned to Oxford this did not prevent a renewal of contact: plainly there were shared interests also. Instead of suffering opprobrium as one hostile to Hopkins' beliefs, Pater – only five years older than Hopkins – wins deference. It shows when Hopkins is retorting to Bridges that he has not been trying to make his friend endure suffering for its own sake (Hopkins had previously written[40] urging Bridges to give to the needy to the point where it 'pinched', the pinching apparently being the main point of the giving). Pater is the man Hopkins chooses as an example of his respect of persons' beliefs:

Can you suppose I should send Pater a discipline wrapped up in a sonnet 'with my best love'? Would it not be mad? And it is much the same to burst upon you with an exhortation to mortification (under the name of 'sensible inconvenience') – which mortification too would be in your case aimless.[41]

Perhaps Hopkins had felt Pater's strength in an area where he himself was acutely sensitive, namely in the relation between art and religion? That possibility must remain conjectural, but on the extent of his antipathy to Pater's philosophy the evidence is clear. It is to be found in Hopkins' undergraduate essay, 'On the probable future of metaphysics'; but, before discussing this, it will be well to give a short account of Pater's thinking to show how the two writers connect.

Pater's habit of rewriting his work again and again was but one sign of the continuous development in his thought. However, it is the early work which concerns us here and the most important sources for his ideas are his review entitled 'Coleridge's Writings' (1866) and his book *The Renaissance* (1873).[42] (His later *Marius the Epicurean* also throws light on this period and his earlier 1864 paper, *Diaphaneité*, – not referred to here - foreshadows some of the ideas present in the works now discussed.)

Implicit in Pater's work is the idea that, because our physical life is continually altering, some corresponding dissolution of moral ideas must take place as well. He says in the Conclusion to *The Renaissance*,

What is the whole physical life in that moment [the moment when someone plunges into water on a hot summer's day] but a combination of natural elements to which science gives their names? But those elements, phosphorus and lime and delicate fibres, are present not in the human body alone: we detect them in places most remote from it. Our physical life is a perpetual motion of them – the passage of the blood, the waste and repairing of the lenses of the eye, the modification of the tissues of the brain under every ray of light and sound – processes which science reduces to simpler and more elementary forces. Like the elements of which we are composed, the actions of those forces extends beyond us: it rusts iron and ripens corn...and birth and gesture and death and the springing of violets from the grave are but a few out of ten thousand resultant combinations. That clear, perpetual outline of face and limb is but an image of ours, under which we group them – a design in a web, the actual threads of which pass out beyond it.[43]

'Perpetual motion', 'ten thousand...combinations' – in short, instability and complexity; but, having invoked the physical sciences so as to reveal this, Pater does not then go on to call on physical laws to return order to the scene. Instead he makes the observer the source of such order as there is, and this in such a way that that order is circumscribed and contingent. In the 'image of ours' 'threads' pass beyond the view of the observer.

The same sequence of thought is to be observed in his review, 'Coleridge's Writings'. 'To the modern spirit,' Pater says, 'nothing is, or can be rightly known except relatively under conditions.'[44] (To digress, the qualifying 'rightly' turns what seems to have the strength of an axiom into a mere point of view; it also makes Pater impregnable, for, though he needs them to establish his own propositions, axioms are, in effect, under his attack.) This is demonstrable from the physical sciences which 'reveal types of life evanescing into each other by inexpressible refinements of change'.[45] It follows, for Pater, that if our physical world is continually altering, so must our moral one be, for 'The moral world is ever in contact with the physical; the relative spirit has invaded moral philosophy from the ground of the inductive science.'[46] Experience is our touchstone, and since experience itself is continually altering, it must therefore deny categories not equally subtle and shifting, deny 'every formula less living and flexible than life itself'.[47] (By this logic, 'Not the fruit of experience, but experience itself, is the end.'[48]) Thus, of the complex relations between man and the world he lives in Pater says:

The truth of these relations experience gives us; not the truth of eternal outlines effected once for all, but a world of fine gradations and subtly linked conditions, shifting intricately as we ourselves change; and bids us by constant clearing of the organs of observation and perfecting of analysis to make what we can of these.[49]

We arrive – as in the Conclusion to *The Renaissance* – at the observer, the individual as the source of order.

From this ground Pater launches his attack on Coleridge. He says:

The literary life of Coleridge was a disinterested struggle against the application of the relative spirit to moral and religious questions. Everywhere he is restlessly scheming to apprehend the absolute; to affirm it effectively; to get it acknowledged.[50]

Pater's feeling of the unworthiness of Coleridge's attempt is given here in that word 'scheming' which suggests, in this context, not simply duplicity but a fundamental untruth to life, an untruth which comes because Coleridge had a 'passion for the absolute, for something fixed where all is moving'.[51]

To return now to Hopkins' undergraduate essay; though Pater is not named by Hopkins it is Pater's philosophy which is chiefly under attack. Before giving 'the probable future of metaphysics' Hopkins characterises contemporary thinking in a way which plainly includes Pater in its scope. He speaks of 'the ideas so rife now of a continuity without fixed points, not to say *saltus* or breaks, of development in one chain of necessity, of species having no absolute types'.[52] He predicts that there will be a return to Platonism or 'more correctly Realism', and speculates that this will challenge 'the prevalent philosophy of continuity or flux' (Pater's philosophy) on three major points:

> The first is that of type of species...The new Realism will maintain that in musical strings the roots of chords, to use technical wording, are mathematically fixed and give a standard by which to fix all the notes of the appropriate scale... so also there are certain forms which have a great hold on the mind and are always reappearing and seem imperishable, such as the designs of Greek vases and lyres, the cone upon Indian shawls, the honeysuckle moulding, the fleur-de-lys...and some pictures we may long look at and never grasp or hold together, while the composition of others strikes the mind with a conception of unity which is never dislodged: and these things are inexplicable on the theory of pure chromatism or continuity – the forms have in some sense or other an absolute existence.[53]

(The comment about unity in pictures is an embryonic statement of 'inscape'.)

It was this absoluteness which Pater denied; it is not the permanence of fixed patterns but the transience of experience which strikes him. Instead of Hopkins' belief that there are 'certain forms which ...seem imperishable' we have his conviction that

> those impressions of the individual mind to which, for each one of us, experience dwindles down, are in perpetual flight; that each of them is limited by time, and that as time is infinitely divisible, each of them is infinitely divisible also; all that is actual in it being a single moment, gone while we try to apprehend it, of which it may ever be more truly said that it has ceased to be than that it is.[54]

Pater's is an evanescent world made of fragments, and these fragments hold no meaning outside themselves, for they are, in endless sequence, only aggregations of experience just as complex. Against this infinite divisibility the undergraduate opposes his second point; we begin with the whole (here, in the form of Platonic Idealism):

> A second point at issue may be the prevalent principle that knowledge is from the birth upwards, is a history of growth, and mounts from the part to the whole. Realism will undoubtedly once more maintain that the Idea is only given...from the whole downwards to the parts.[55]

Such a dissemination from the centre gives reality an order and meaning outside that imposed by the individual.

We have already seen that Pater's order is locked in the mind of the observer; so his Marius 'was to continue all through life, something of an idealist, constructing the world for himself in great measure from within, by the exercise of meditative power'.[56] The image of the individual's confinement recurs in Pater's work. In *The Renaissance* each mind keeps 'as a solitary prisoner its own dream of a world'.[57] Marius reasons 'that we are never to get beyond the walls of the closely shut cell of one's own personality'.[58] Again Hopkins resists the idea of individual dominance by invoking the principle of a central unity in reality:

A form of atomism like a stiffness or sprain seems to hang upon and hamper our speculation: it is an over-powering, a disproportioned sense of personality... The new school of metaphysics will probably encounter this atomism of personality with some shape of the Platonic Ideas.[59]

Instead of arbitrariness, fixity; instead of the fragmentary, the organic; instead of the personal, the absolute; and the final rebuttal of all that Pater stood for might seem to have been Hopkins' entry, in 1866, into the Catholic Church of which, in the same year, Pater was saying this:

The Catholic church and humanity are two powers that divide the intellect and spirit of man. On the Catholic side is faith, rigidly logical as Ultramontanism, with a proportion of the facts of life, that is, all that is despairing in life coming naturally under its formula. On the side of humanity is all that is desirable in the world, all that is sympathetic with its laws, and succeeds through that sympathy.[60]

Religion, which is, in this passage from 'Coleridge's Writings', a 'formula' to satisfy the despairing, has in Pater's essay on Winckelmann (1867) a base in a care for 'charms and talismans'[61] (by which disdain he makes faith not simply a mistaken alternative to his philosophy but discreditable as well). Between the insouciance of Pater's 'not disquieting oneself' and the religious ardour which took Hopkins into the priesthood there could be no communion, and this difference powerfully affected their beliefs about the relation between art and life, but there is striking kinship in the way they both preserve the autonomy of a work of art.

Pater's view of the relation between form and content in his essay 'The School of Giorgione' (1877) is of a kind which sets art outside the reach of system or dogma. It receives its most eloquent expression in this famous passage:

All art constantly aspires towards the condition of music. For while in all other kinds of art it is possible to distinguish the matter from the form, and the understanding can always make this distinction, yet it is the constant effort of art to obliterate it. That the mere matter of a poem, for instance, its subject, namely its

given incidents or situation – that the mere matter of a picture, the actual circumstances of an event, the actual topography of a landscape – should be nothing
without the form, the spirit, of the handling, that this form, this mode of handling, should become an end in itself, should penetrate every part of the matter: this
is what all art constantly strives after, and achieves in different degrees.[62]

Now compare Hopkins, writing in February 1868, and giving –
already giving, as early as this – his own distinctive formulation of
the same idea:

The further in anything, as in a work of art, the organisation is carried out, the
deeper the form penetrates, the prepossession flushes the matter, the more
effort will be required in apprehension, the more power of comparison, the more
capacity for receiving that synthesis of (either successive or spatially distinct)
impressions which gives us the unity with the prepossession conveyed by it.[63]

Not a line of the poetry he had written to this date and which is
extant would be generally acknowledged to present readers with the
difficulties of his mature work, and yet the theory behind and the
defence for the difficulty is already formulated: 'the deeper the form
penetrates...the more effort will be required in apprehension'.

Form penetrating matter: the wording is Pater's as we can see,
although Hopkins' use antedates Pater's published statement by
nine years. Such a concurrence of view does at least raise the possibility of fruitful interchange between the two men on this subject,
though this is not something on which much weight can be rested.
The broader significance of the agreement lies in the alignment
which by its attention to form resists the pressure of contemporary
orthodoxies to make art tritely moralising. Such a focus as these two
statements share keeps poetry free of subservience to received
dogmas because its *raison d'être* is placed elsewhere. However, the
risk entailed is that of the shedding of responsibility, inasmuch as
'responsibility' is out-goingness and the sort of art envisaged here is
not established in terms of its connection with the mundane world.
For Pater the risk was very real: conspicuously in his early work art
was a surrogate religion, a gratification in the ineffable. Pater's 'the
supreme, artistic view of life'[64] is the result of a confusion in which
Hopkins was incapable of sharing, however. His Catholicism stopped
him; so also did his hold on the real. Hopkins' comments on 'form'
are not confined to art; they may be true of 'anything'.

Indeed, this was the crucial distinction between the two men in intellectual terms. Pater was surrounded by a world full of beautiful creations with no significance outside themselves; Hopkins was part of a beautiful Creation. For him the 'form' of art was to be found in nature. Thus he notes in his Journal 'A budded lime against the field wall: turn, pose, and counterpoint in the twigs and buds – the *form* speaking',[65] and (in 1874), 'I looked at some delicate flying shafted ashes – there was one especially of single sonnet-like inscape.'[66] In the unhindered natural world form penetrates matter with its own deep meaning, and Hopkins was to say in one of his most revealing comments on the relation between visible beauty and moral truth, 'All the world is full of inscape and chance left free to act falls into an order as well as purpose.'[67] The world is there for scrutiny and investigation. 'For a certain time', he writes in an early letter to Baillie (1863), 'I am astonished at the beauty of a tree, shape, effect etc, then when the passion, so to speak, has subsided, it is consigned to my treasury of explored beauty'.[68] Nature presents him with problems to solve – bluebells 'baffle you with their inscape',[69] the 'spraying' of beech woods is 'baffling and beautiful'[70] – for the appearance holds a reality which is there to be grasped. In all his attempts there is energy and purposefulness: (of a river) 'by watching hard the banks began to sail upstream, the scaping unfolded';[71] (in spring) 'This is the time to study inscape in the spraying of trees, for the swelling buds carry them to a pitch which the eye could not else gather.'[72] Because, chronologically, Hopkins was in the wake of the Romantic movement it is easy to ignore the fact that his attitude to nature has more in common with that of the naturalist than with that of Wordsworth, for example.

Pater, however, lives amongst mysteries which he cherishes *as* mysteries. They take him away from the commonplace. He loves the esoteric. Leonardo da Vinci is thus described:

Poring over his crucibles, making experiments with colour, trying, by a strange variation of the alchemist's dream, to discover the secret, not of an elixir to make man's natural life immortal, but of giving immortality to the subtlest and most delicate effects of painting, he seemed to them rather the sorcerer or the magician, possessed of curious secrets and a hidden knowledge, living in a world of which he alone possessed the key.[73]

'Strange', 'secret', 'subtle', 'curious', 'hidden' – these are some of

Pater's favourite words because they are a continual acknowledgement of the elusiveness of life, but the reference to Leonardo's gift of immortality hints at another function: they mark the way out of that elusiveness, the means of escape from ordinariness.

It is others who are responsible for that release into the perpetual sublime, not oneself in one's life of contemplation. Of this Edward Thomas says:

> It is impossible not to regard this aim, as Pater expressed it, as a kind of higher philately or connoisseurship. He speaks like a collector of the great and beautiful ...Thus he tends to conventionalise the strange, to turn all things great and small into a coldly pathetic strain of music. He refines upon the artists who have refined upon the Lord of Lords. Shakespeare's Claudio is a 'flowerlike young man' set in 'the horrible blackness' of a prison; Isabella is 'clear, detached, columnar,' or, with the Duke as friar, 'like some grey monastic picture.' He is very glad of those who do not make 'impassioned contemplation' their end. For they are the chief contrivers of the spectacles which he is looking on at, with appropriate emotions; and but for them, contemplation could hardly be of 'supreme importance' in the conduct of life, since all would be contemplative, and there would be little to contemplate, save the artist Death, 'blanching the features of youth and spoiling its goodly hair.'[74]

Thomas describes Pater's dependent position, and the consequent flaw in his approach: the passive lover of art cannot logically exalt his own passivity to pre-eminence when it depends for its worth on the activity of others, the artists. Pater deals in his own kind of immortality (Mona Lisa has 'a perpetual life'[75]) and in a manner which disvalues present and particular experiences. These 'morsels of actual life' must be 'refined upon or idealised',[76] and a great picture is a play of sunlight and shadow 'but refined upon, and dealt with more subtly and exquisitely than by nature itself'.[77]

Pater's stricture on Coleridge might be repeated at this point: he had a 'passion for the absolute, for something fixed where all is moving'. So did Pater; except that in him this is disguised. He separates art and life, and in such a manner that, while life moves, art provides a sanctuary from its turbulence. Artistic genius puts 'a happy world of its own creation in place of the meaner world of our common days'[78] (note the prescription that the world be happy, and the words 'in place of' – Pater is not speaking simply of the autonomy of art). Modern art can 'give the spirit at least an equivalent for the sense of freedom',[79] which freedom the revelations of modern science (from whose inductive base Pater has already attacked Coleridge) have deprived us of for ever, 'That naive, rough sense of freedom, which supposes man's will to be limited, if at all, only by a will stronger than his.'[80] How remarkable this is! Pater is almost regretting the passing of belief in God, because in its place has come something more insidious and confining. Necessity is not an external force, it is within us in the determining material of which we are made. Life is not dynamic and full, it is derivative at its best, justified by art: 'Who, if he saw through all,' asks Pater, writing in connection with the achievements of contemporary art, 'would fret against the chain of circumstances which endows one at the end with those great experiences?'[81] Here (at the end of the essay on Winckelmann) Pater's refusal to acknowledge the activeness of the creative artist and his engagement with that very life from which Pater himself sought to retire is at its most extreme. His intelligence takes a sterile course. The flight of a falcon, or thick clusters of stars, one is led to believe, can be important to him only in art or poetry.

Hopkins developed his own interest in form characteristically in the direction of law and strictness; he invented the word 'inscape' to help him do so. Perceiving the inscape in something seems for him to have been the important first step in discovering the ideal in the visible world; it was not that discovery itself but a precondition. It seems that he saw inscape as existing in different degrees. It is this fact together with the variety of contexts in which the term is used rather than any conceptual difficulty which causes discussion of its meaning.

Since the word first occurs in the place where 'instress' is also first used it is convenient to consider the two terms together. In Hopkins' notes on Parmenides (in a notebook dated 9 February 1868) we have this comment on the Greek philosopher:

His feeling for instress, for the flush and foredrawn, and for inscape / is most striking and from this one can understand Plato's reverence for him as the great father of Realism.[82]

In the same notes Hopkins speaks subsequently of feeling 'the depth of an instress' and of feeling 'how fast the inscape holds a thing'. These terms can thus be defined by deducing their meaning from context and from parenthesis. Immediately before Hopkins' first mention of 'instress' he makes the comment that Parmenides' fragments are difficult to translate satisfactorily 'in a subjective or in a wholly outward sense'. I take it that Hopkins' parenthesis 'the flush and foredrawn' preserves this fusion of an inner activity (in the observer) with an external reality. 'Flush' seems to have the sense of a rush of feeling or vigour, and we are helped with 'foredrawn' by Hopkins' subsequent mention of 'the mind's grasp – the foredrawing act': in other words 'instress' is a rush of feeling which comes in the making contact with external reality – as if in deep recognition of something out there, a sort of correspondence between 'me' and 'it'.

Hopkins seems to have coined the word 'instress' only at that date, for the notes immediately prior to those on Parmenides show him in need of such a term. He speaks there of the mind having two sorts of energy; one is a transitional kind, where one thought follows another in the reasoning process, and the other is 'an abiding kind for which I remember no name, in which the mind is absorbed (as far as that may be), taken up by, dwells upon, enjoys, a single thought'.[83] (Though Hopkins tries to match the word 'contemplation' to this second kind of energy he is evidently dissatisfied with this.) The origin of the word 'instress' seems, then, to owe something to Hopkins' feelings about art, for he continues in the same notes, 'Art exacts this energy of contemplation.' The same may also be claimed for 'inscape' which, inasmuch as it 'holds a thing' fast, seems to be foreshadowed in his comments on how organisation is carried out in a work of art and how form penetrates matter.

Whether this is true or not, Hopkins freely applies the word 'inscape' to both art and nature. From the time of his visit to Switzerland (July 1868) onwards it is in frequent use in his Journal in connection with, for example, plants, trees, mountains, clouds, flowers, and horses. It is also used of architecture, and then, in June 1874, employed in connection with an art exhibition where he speaks, for example, of 'inscape of composition'.[84] In his Lecture-notes 'Poetry and Verse', which may be dated between September 1873 and July 1874, Hopkins describes poetry as speech 'employed to carry the inscape of speech for the inscape's sake'.[85] Thus we have

quite firmly established in the years of silence the view which
Hopkins was later to repeat in his letters – to Bridges in 1879,
'design, pattern, or what I am in the habit of calling 'inscape' is
what I above all aim at in poetry';[86] and to Dixon in 1886, '*inscape*'
is 'the very soul of art'.[87] It is the range of applications to which
Hopkins puts the word which gives rise to difficulties in interpretation. If one were to substitute 'form' for the term it would be clear
how elastic that would have to be to encompass (e.g.) both form of a
tree and form of speech. Hopkins did not feel the strain; his use of
'inscape' instead of 'form' is part of the reason.

David Downes presents cogently the probable reasoning behind
the term:

it is clear that the prefix 'in' of 'inscape' denotes that 'scape' is the outer fixed
shape of the intrinsic form of a thing. For that reason Hopkins was not satisfied
with the terms design and pattern as the unqualified designation of the intrinsic
order of being. These terms indicate an order impressed from without, an
extrinsic principle of unity.[88]

As an alternative to 'design' or 'pattern', 'form' risks describing the
mere appearance of a thing which because it is an appearance is
subject to change. Moreover, 'form' implies something outward
only; 'inscape' insists on an abiding and essential quality which
shows itself in externals but which, unlike them, has permanence.
Thus Hopkins notes of a painting, 'Intense expression of face,
expression of character, not mood, true inscape.'[89] 'Character' in
this sense, which not only implies distinctive features but can also
take on in some contexts the additional sense of inner moral qualities,
is probably the closest word which could be offered as a synonym for
'inscape'. It allows one to acknowledge that there are different sorts
of inscape: Hopkins speaks of 'a beautiful inscape',[90] 'a broad careless inscape',[91] and 'strongly inscaped leaves',[92] amongst many
other usages.

'Form' or 'inscape' is for Hopkins the essential bridge between
matter and the immaterial. It is not in itself matter for it needs a
discerning eye to see it, nor is it exclusively mental, for it has its
existence in the object seen. It is clear, though, from the many often
casual references which Hopkins' Journal makes to 'inscape' that an
educated eye – the eye of an artist or sculptor – is the primary

requirement for its discovery. For Hopkins its discovery is charged
with potential, the sort of potential realised (in 1870) in his famous
claim for the bluebell: 'I do not think I have ever seen anything
more beautiful than the bluebell I have been looking at. I know the
beauty of our Lord by it.'[93] His word 'inscape' permanently holds
out the possibility of an insight into the unity of things; this is why
he is able to employ it so widely.

In the summer of 1872 Hopkins began to read the lengthy *Opus
Oxoniense* of the medieval schoolman John Duns Scotus and wrote
excitedly in a much-quoted Journal entry of 3 August that 'just then
when I took in any inscape of the sky or sea I thought of Scotus'.[94]
There is the merest shift in meaning between Hopkins' 1870 note
about knowing Christ's beauty *by* that of a bluebell and his Journal
entry four years later about a starlit sky and 'our Lord *to* and *in* whom
all that beauty comes home'[95] (my italics), but such slender though
important prepositional changes are signs of the strengthening in him
of the central confidence of those nature poems which followed the
breaking of his silence, signs of the effect on him of reading Scotus.
I take these two Journal entries and the notes on Parmenides
(mentioned in connection with 'inscape' and referred to below) as
being the chief *loci* for understanding that this was a matter of
development, not of departure. As often, Hopkins was already close
to anticipating the direction encouraged in him by his reading.
    In the sonnet 'Duns Scotus's Oxford' Hopkins described the
philosopher as the most distinctive 'unraveller' of what is real. That,
and Hopkins' sigh to Patmore (explicitly connected with Scotus)
that 'it is all one almost to be too full of meaning and to have none
and to see very deep and not to see at all',[96] ought to act as cautions
about the kind of help we can expect from him in understanding
Hopkins' poetry, for 'unravelling' is a method quite different from
Hopkins' own characteristic compression and, if a poem is successful, it will itself carry within it the main force of its own semantic
charge. It is mistaken to suppose that Scotus has some proprietorial
right over Hopkins. We may say that he encouraged what was
Franciscan in Hopkins, encouraged him, that is, more towards
matters of trust than towards those of abnegation.

What Hopkins appears to believe after reading him is that the mind, disconnected from what he had called its 'transitional' roles (one such role would be the 'consequitive reasoning' which Keats disparaged)[97] and allowed to dwell, would turn naturally to the source of its own being. Such a disconnection, a dwelling on, does of course take place in the taking in of an inscape. In special moments one might have a glimpse of oneself making such an intuitive return. Hence this in 'The Handsome Heart':

> What the heart is! which, like carriers let fly –
> Doff darkness, homing nature knows the rest –
> To its own fine function, wild and self-instressed,
> Falls light as ten years long taught how to and why.

The fundamental harmony which such a view supposes between observer and observed, individual and world, is particularly evident in the Welsh poems where Christ, ground of one's being, 'under the world's splendour and wonder', is wafted from the starlight ('The Wreck of the Deutschland', stanza 5) and 'gleaned' from the clouds ('Hurrahing in Harvest'); but the convictions that 'mortal beauty... keeps warm / Men's wits to the things that are', and that beauty is 'home at heart' ('To what serves Mortal Beauty?'), and that man in his finest moments when he is truest to his nature exemplifies Christ just as Christ exemplifies him ('As kingfishers catch fire', 'The Soldier'), remained with him into later life.

To return for a moment to the notes on Parmenides: what chiefly interests Hopkins there is the help the Greek philosopher can give him in understanding what makes it possible for the outer world of material things to come into one's consciousness (which 'coming' is not, of course, simply a matter of receiving images on the retina); what, in other words, enables one to say of something, 'it is'. The quality of 'being' is what both the mind and the perceived object share, and without this connection

There would be no bridge, no stem of stress between us and things to bear us out and carry the mind over: without stress we might not and could not say / Blood is red / but only / This blood is red / or / The last blood I saw was red / nor even that, for in later language not only universals would not be true but the copula would break down even in particular judgments.[98]

Hopkins' thought is very compressed here because it develops as he writes, sometimes overtaking what has come earlier. He says, in effect, that without the mind's supplying something in the act of perception, and thus acting as something other than a merely passive receptor, it would be impossible for it to make statements, whether these statements are general (blood is red) or specific (this blood is red). The general statement would be impossible because the general term 'blood' (i.e. all blood) involves more than one has in front of one. The specific statement would be impossible because the kind of recognition (and hence prior, remembered experience of 'redness') which 'red' involves is also not something provided exclusively by the object in front of one; though, when Hopkins speaks of the copula breaking down, he seems to have in mind not this reason but the more general fact that saying 'is' of something is the supplying of a connection between that and the rest of reality. (Setting aside considerations of truth and falsity, a predicate, if it is to be meaningful, cannot be something which is of its nature affirmable only of one subject.) However, that even to say 'red' of something would be impossible without the 'stress' Hopkins is speaking of seems to be allowed for by his saying subsequently in the same notes: 'The truth in thought is Being, stress, and each word is one way of acknowledging Being.' Such an acknowledging does not need the object to be before the mind, for (Hopkins translates): 'Look at it, though absent, yet to the mind's eye as fast present here; for absence cannot break off Being from its hold on Being.' Consciousness carries the object about even when it is 'unextended'. In this form the object is 'foredrawn' or, as we would usually say, we have an idea of it, and 'Parmenides will say that the mind's grasp – νοεῖν, the foredrawing act – that this is blood or that that blood is red is to be looked for in Being, the foredrawn, alone, not in the thing we named blood or the blood we worded as being red.' According to Parmenides, says Hopkins, it is in the quality of Being that the essential connection is established, and not because of something in the object or of something in the form of words we used to describe it.

This view of Being as the fundamental truth contains the possibility of comprehending the unity of all things, material and immaterial alike. It is endorsed by Scotus in such a way as to develop this possibility for a Christian. Being applies in an identical sense to God and to his creatures, to the infinite and the finite, to spiritual and material. Being is distinguished only from Not-being, for if there were any other determination in Being it would not be possible to speak meaningfully of God's existence (thus the Thomist analogical knowledge of God's existence, where God exists in a manner *like* other sorts but – because he is God – differently, is no knowledge at all): Being is univocal.

Being, for Scotus, is also metaphysically prior to its particular manifestations (in the sense that it is true of God, of course it must be). It is not limited by any categories such as those of substance or quantity; these it transcends.

However, some sort of contraction of Being must obviously take place if there are to be particulars. Such a contraction, a contraction of the common nature which all individuals of one species share, occurs by virtue of a number of forms which are formally distinct from one another (as God's will is from God's intelligence) but which are not separate in actuality because such a separation would deny the unity of the individual (one cannot separate Socrates' humanity from Socrates, though 'humanity' is recognisably distinct, a contraction of Being). The final determinant of individuality, however, is the mysterious quality of *haecceitas* or 'thisness' which belongs uniquely to one individual.

Scotus' ontology sees the world's being as contingent on God's necessary being and as an expression of God's will untramelled by any other consideration. Against the resulting criticism of him that he introduced a moral arbitrariness into ethics it has been said[99] that Scotus' voluntarism does not in fact allow for God to act capriciously in his own essence. As Hopkins read him, however, there is at least a possibility that he encouraged in the zealous novice that simple adoration of power which upsets some stanzas in 'The Wreck of the Deutschland'.

Before turning from this outline – necessary for an understanding of Scotus' epistemology, which seems to have been what Hopkins first found attractive in him – it is important to add that the schoolman taught that Christ's incarnation was willed independently of sin. (In my view we meet this teaching specifically in stanzas 6 and 7 of

'The Wreck of the Deutschland'.) It was the completion of God's work in creation and only because of sin did his incarnation take on a redemptive role as well and hence involve his crucifixion. Christ is the consummation of created nature; for humanity he is the ideal, the complete form of which mankind has only partial shares. Scotus also championed the doctrine of the Immaculate Conception, notably at the University of Paris.

The distinction which Scotus makes between the general – the common nature – and the particular – the *haecceitas* – is reflected in his account of perception, where he distinguishes between the innate power of knowing, capable of operating independently of man's conscious instruction, and the will-directed intelligence. The former concerns itself intuitively, unconsciously, with Being as such (and thus – connecting this with Hopkins' Parmenides notes – supplies that energy which enables one to say 'it is'), and responds to what is undetermined. The latter is an expression of selfhood and produces distinct understanding; its knowledge is acquired, whereas the former appears to be in possession of knowledge already, a memory, albeit confused. Scotus says that one can catch this innate power at work, for example in that phenomenon (now known as *déjà vu*) which consists in an uncanny sense of having experienced a given set of circumstances at some time previously, even where such previous experience seems to have been impossible, as though one had exactly lived out such a moment before outside one's conscious knowledge and were now disturbed by an untraceable recognition.

Such an innate power appears to reach back in time (supposing, for a moment, that creation were temporal) to the formal constituents of creation. Father Devlin observes: 'The essential whole which the object imposes on my mind is found to break up into parts which tally exactly with distinctions already latent and rooted in my unconscious mind, i.e. my knowing nature.'[100] Such a moment of recognition between 'me' and 'it' in our common origin (one which makes statements exclusively about 'it' or exclusively about 'me' inadequate because of their exclusiveness) is, I think, contained in the contentious tercet of 'The Windhover' and, if so, goes far to account for the difficulty of that poem. Further, it seems to me that often when Hopkins in his poems referred to his 'heart' he was referring to this innate power, to the intuitive movement in his very nature ('homing nature') over which as such he had no control and which directed him to what he saw as the ground of his existence, pure being, his God (e.g. in stanza 18 of 'The Wreck of the Deutschland', 'mother of being in me, heart').

In the sonnet 'Duns Scotus's Oxford' Scotus was for Hopkins the one 'who of all men most sways my spirits to peace', and that, in my view, was the philosopher's most important function for the poet. Scotus had reassured him that man's intuitive sympathetic movement toward the sensible world, since it was outside man's volition, was not a matter either of sin or of merit, for only willed activity can be that. Hence Hopkins' saying in his most doctrinal fragment, 'On a Piece of Music',

> Therefore this masterhood,
> This piece of perfect song,
> This fault-not-found-with good
> Is neither right nor wrong.

In art men, if they are good painters or poets or musicians, simply show what they are; and that activity is morally neutral. As he had it in some notes on Ignatius' *Spiritual Exercises*,

But MEN OF GENIUS ARE SAID TO CREATE, a painting, a poem, a tale, a tune, a policy; not indeed the colours and the canvas, not the words or notes, but the design, the character, the air, the plan. How then? – from themselves, from their own minds. And they themselves, their minds and all, are creatures of God: if the tree created much more the flower and the fruit.[101]

The same sort of involuntariness is indicated in the note Hopkins wrote to Bridges on the closing lines of 'Henry Purcell'. 'The thought is that as the seabird...unaware gives you a whiff of knowledge about his plumage, the marking of which stamps his species...so Purcell, seemingly intent only on the thought or feeling he is to express or call out, incidentally lets you remark the individualising marks of his own genius.'[102] Our knowledge, Scotus had taught him, is of particular individuals; it is by reacting to these in their individuality and concreteness that we come to know generally – a process applicable to poetry as to any other experience.

The poetic outcome of the philosophy of form whose development

I have traced here, with its fusion of the ideal and the real, is 'The Windhover'.

This poem has become the crossword puzzle of English letters, made such because a blurring on the reader's part of the meaning of one word puts the meaning of others, and hence of the whole poem, in doubt, so numerous are the offered alternatives. 'The Windhover' does have a damaging change in direction in the final tercet and also other blemishes, but many of the difficulties of interpretation have been imported. It was written in May 1877, and in September of that year Hopkins tried with less success to do the same sort of thing again. It is helpful to look at the later poem first.

As in 'The Windhover' so in 'Hurrahing in Harvest' Hopkins is trying to show the active moment when some part of nature is sensed not only in its usual (public) form but also in simultaneous and private perception as the actual presence of Christ. As on earth so in the sky all is beautiful abundance; the heavenward 'rise' of the stooks, the 'meal' that links sky-vapour to earth's grain, and the 'sack' clouds that figure the garnering, anticipate the 'lifting up' of the second quatrain. The whole of the octave awaits the climactic union of heaven and earth. This union is realised in the later poem's sestet:

> And the azurous hung hills are his world-wielding shoulder
> Majestic – as a stallion stalwart, very-violet-sweet! –
> These things, these things were here and but the beholder
> Wanting; which two when they once meet,
> The heart rears wings bold and bolder
> And hurls for him, O half hurls earth for him off under his feet.

A single image underlies the thought of this stanza. It is of winged Pegasus, initially at rest but possessed of enormous latent power, at last taking off in an immense skyward thrust.[103] (Other elements are present as well, but in such a compressed way that one is inclined to suppose – wrongly – that they should fuse together instead of being taken consecutively. Blue sky hangs like a drape above and behind hills which ripple the surface of the earth as the shoulder-bones of the Pegasus–stallion ripple the animal's hide, suggestive of its underlying strength. The bluish purple of these hills is reminiscent of the colour of violets, and thus recalls that flower's sweet smell. So the compacted thought may be reasoned out.) The stallion image is discovered first in the inert hills, majestically still but in fact 'world-wielding'. Then observer and observed meet, and the same image, further developed now in the full active power of the rearing creature, becomes a way of expressing that delight which indeed wholly takes over the beholder in the rush of upward movement. The poem finishes in pure ecstatic motion which loses the distinction we would customarily insist on between what is seen and the person who sees it. Nonetheless, the stallion image *has* been transposed from perceived to perceiver, and one can detect the change. What happens in the sestet of 'The Windhover' is that this transposition is no longer evident: the connection between what is perceived and the way it is perceived becomes absolute.

Hopkins overcomes the problem of acknowledging the difference between the public presence and the private vision in 'The Windhover' by a shift in tense. The poem is about a memory of 'this morning', but the paradoxical thing about memories is that they are always in the present: a memory allows for simultaneity of then and now.

The Windhover: to Christ our Lord

I caught this morning morning's minion, king-
    dom of daylight's dauphin, dapple-dawn-drawn Falcon, in his riding
    Of the rolling level underneath him steady air, and striding
High there, how he rung upon the rein of a wimpling wing
In his ecstasy! then off, off forth on swing,
    As a skate's heel sweeps smooth on a bow-bend: the hurl and gliding
    Rebuffed the big wind. My heart in hiding
Stirred for a bird, – the achieve of, the mastery of the thing!

Brute beauty and valour and act, oh, air, pride, plume, here
    Buckle! AND the fire that breaks from thee then, a billion
Times told lovelier, more dangerous, O my chevalier!

    No wonder of it: shéer plód makes plough down sillion
Shine, and blue-bleak embers, ah my dear,
    Fall, gall themselves, and gash gold-vermilion.

The vision of the falcon, his very being 'caught this morning', 'striding / High there' in the sky, is re-created 'here' in the remembering of it. However, the vision is, in a manner, public, because anyone could have seen the same bird movements (though they

might not have 'caught' them as Hopkins did); the remembering in
the sestet is obviously private – Hopkins does it. Moreover past and
present in memory are differently constructed: the first is sequential
with the bird riding in the air, ringing round, then swinging off; the
second happens in a moment on the word 'buckle'. The first has a
series of physical details of wing movements in the air which
approach abstraction in that the excitement is so plainly with the
patterns thus made and the pre-eminence in the air which they
express, rather than with any bodily existence independent of
motion (the octave is, for example, entirely without colour, always
sparingly used by the mature Hopkins but here notably absent, even
in 'dapple-dawn' where one might expect it). In the second, truly
abstract qualities are pulled together in the syntax that fastens them
in 'buckle': the abstractions are actively realised in the remembering
of the bird flight. In short, we ought to be sensitive to the fact that,
though the experience of the sestet has definition only because of
what has preceded it in the octave, it is not a summary or duplication
of the first eight lines. That summary has already been given in 'My
heart in hiding / Stirred for a bird, – the achieve of, the mastery of
the thing!'

'Buckle' in the sestet has a meaning not to be plotted simply by
recourse to a dictionary. In part it does what any verb at the end of a
list of nouns would do, whatever that verb's actual meaning: it
draws those terms together and invites us to consider some quality
they share (paradoxically, it might even be the quality of flying
apart). 'Beauty' and 'valour' and the other abstract qualities
separately indicated in the list which opens the stanza are thus joined
in the mind's re-creation of the experience of 'this morning'. But
'buckle' also mimics the action of the falling embers in the poem's
last line: these qualities *yield* – the best synonym for 'buckle'. The
new analysis results in a new synthesis of perception; the display of
valour and pride and the rest is made possible only by the collapse
of these separate ideal categories in the real particular, the bird. The
flying falcon, by being wholly and concentratedly itself in its own
activity, gives out the essential truth in things (just as the plough in
its activity and the embers in theirs do), and to realise that truth is
to understand it as being in oneself as well as out there. 'AND'

emphasises this – in capitals too forceful for the reader's comfort –
by extending the control of 'buckle' to the fire which results from
it as well as to the abstractions which have preceded it in the poem.
When Christ's active presence is perceived in the bird, the 'chevalier'
(now both Christ and the falcon - their identities are indistinguishable in so far as Christ's being includes the bird's also) is 'a billion /
Times told lovelier' than the bird was before Christ's presence in it
had been grasped.

It is a sign of the extraordinary accomplishment of the poem that
the stresses in the opening part of the sestet build up to an explosion
on the powerful first syllable of 'Buckle!' which is semantically the
climactic moment. The truth and ecstasy at the truth are thus
realised together. After this acknowledgement it seems carping to
say that nonetheless there are irritating blemishes in the achievement. There is an obvious awkwardness about 'rolling level', which
can be analysed into good sense (waves or hills, for example, roll
level in that their general plane is not tilted), but at the expense of
common association which makes 'level' mean flat and 'rolling'
mean the opposite. 'More dangerous' is unsatisfying because of its
inadequately announced arrival: unlike loveliness (with whose
comparative it is paired) 'danger' is not one of the parameters of the
poem. (I take the phrase to refer to the terrifying immediacy of
Christ in the falcon, but this does not make its introduction any less
intrusive.) Further, Hopkins loses some control by his introduction
in the last tercet of the idea that destruction can be beautiful. He
speaks of a plough polished by the earth through which it passes,[104]
and of coals falling in a grate and giving off vivid coruscations of
flame, and says that, in view of these occurrences, the fire from the
falcon is not surprising. But 'plod' and 'gash' introduce elements
not so far present, and leave as an open question the problem of the
way they are to be related to the experiences the poem primarily
describes. We may be helped, in an external way, by the knowledge
that Hopkins saw Christ's incarnation as itself a sacrifice of personal
interest in the Son; but this does not in the poem close the gap
between destruction and creation. It was quite in character for
Hopkins at the time he wrote 'The Windhover' to find beauty in
self-sacrifice and to see God's purpose in destruction (we have this

view in 'The Wreck of the Deutschland' and it harms that poem as well as this one); the consequence here is that a kind of short-circuit occurs between laboriousness and self-sacrifice and 'more dangerous', and draws the ingenuity of commentators in the direction of allegory, a course they are further encouraged on by the implicit comparison of Christ (not now the lord in triumph, but broken in his Passion – 'ah my dear') with the gashed embers. The poem is thus made into an image for a lifetime – Hopkins' lifetime – and one to be construed at will. In part the temptation arises because critics have brought with them their own notions of success and failure rather than accept Hopkins' less palatable ones. It arises also because of a fault in the poem: Hopkins has not answered our need to reconcile his thought on immolation with his feeling of ecstasy. The poem's orchestration changes: it finishes diminuendo, the sound-pattern adding to the last brilliant disintegration the sense of expiration.

The foregoing account does, of course, cover some very contentious areas, so I now give the reasoning which underlies it. It seems to me that it is important, firstly, to correct two sometimes unspoken assumptions which have often proved misleading: that seeing a windhover in flight was a new experience for Hopkins and hence a challenge to him,[105] and, connected with that, the assumption that the sighting was involuntary, that the initiative was with the bird to whose sudden appearance Hopkins felt the need to respond. There is a need to set a true context.

The second of the two assumptions (that the sighting is rare or unique) is the more simply refuted of the two so I take that first. Hopkins was no stranger in 1877 to the sight of flying falcons. In 1872 on holiday in the Isle of Man he records in his Journal, 'a big hawk flew down chasing a little shrieking bird close beside us'.[106] In the same month, August, he has the note, 'We saw hawks and gulls and cormorants and a heron, I think.'[107] The following year he returned to the Isle of Man and, coming back from Snae Fell, 'we saw eight or perhaps ten hawks together'.[108] In the summer of 1874 he was in Devon and saw that 'a hawk also was hanging on the hover',[109] and when, in September of that year, he went to St Beuno's to study theology, one of his first entries reads:

For the first time to the Rock. The Rock is a great resort of hawks and owls.[110]

One may fairly infer from this that, in Wales, he could see falcons
virtually any time he wished, and that this was so is, I think, confirmed by a very wistful remark in a letter to his father just before he
left St Beuno's:

No sooner were we among the Welsh hills than I saw the hawks flying and other
pleasant sights soon to be seen no more.[111]

Seeing a falcon in 1877 would not then, of itself, have been a special
event for Hopkins, yet the octave of 'The Windhover' plainly deals
with a remarkable experience: what was it?

The answer lies in the words 'I caught' which open the poem, and
these, properly understood, oppose the second mistaken assumption
which I identified above – that the initiative is with the bird. However, these words are usually neglected or taken to mean, in the
words of one anthology editor's gloss, 'caught a glimpse of'. In fact,
when Hopkins' frequent sightings of flying falcons are connected
with other Journal entries, it becomes clear that the experience of
'The Windhover' is not the product of a casual glimpse but of a
purposeful effort on the poet's part.

'I caught' signifies the desired grasp of something recondite, and
Hopkins' use of 'catch' and 'caught' with this sense is well established
before 1877. In 1871 he writes about clouds:

May 24 – At sunset and later a strongly marked moulded rack. I made out the
make of it, thus [there is a small sketch in the Journal] – cross hatching in fact. . .
Since that day [a reference to April 21] and since this (May 24) I have noticed
this kind of cloud: its brindled and hatched scaping though difficult to catch is
remarkable when seen. . . Today (July 7) there has been much of this cloud and
its make easily read.[112]

Hopkins is not talking here about immediate appearances. His
references to the difficulty of catching the cloud's 'scaping' and to
the fact that he 'made out the make of it' show that he is trying to
uncover the essential pattern (characteristically, as an artist, he
reproduces it – in a sketch which has no immediate likeness to a
cloud formation). In 1872, in an entry about wave movements,
'catch' is used again, and in a context which likewise suggests the
grasping of something elusive after long study:

About all the turns of the scaping from the break and flooding of wave to its run
out again I have not yet satisfied myself. The shores are swimming and the eyes

have before them a region of milky surf but it is hard for them to unpack the huddling and knarls of the water and law out the shapes and sequence of the running: I catch however the looped or forked wisp made by every big pebble the backwater runs over[113]

Hopkins' effort is to 'law out' shapes and distinguish their order in time, and this he fails in; but he does 'catch' the pattern made when wave water runs over a stone back to the body of the sea.

Two more examples occur in entries for 1873. In February, writing at Stonyhurst about inscape and the way the world always has order if chance is not interfered with, Hopkins says:

looking out of my window I caught it in the random clods and broken heaps of snow made by the cast of a broom.[114]

Later in the year, of bluebells in a nearby wood he was to write:

I caught as well as I could while my companions talked the Greek rightness of their beauty, the lovely / what people call / 'gracious' bidding one to another. . . and a notable glare the eye may abstract and sever from the blue colour / of light beating up from so many glassy heads, which like water is good to float their deeper instress in upon the mind.[115]

There is present here not only the same sense of difficulty in apprehension (Hopkins' companions are a distraction to him) but also, as with his comments on the waves, a strong awareness of his own activity as an observer. 'The eye may abstract', and, in this instance, the mind's involvement is deeper if it does.

Two further instances may be taken as confirming the idea that Hopkins' use of 'caught' is quite distinctive when it is related to the act of seeing, and also as suggesting a close involvement of 'catching' with the process of artistic creation. Firstly, from 1874 (Hopkins was teaching rhetoric at the time at Roehampton, near London):

April 6 – Sham fight on the Common, 7000 men, chiefly volunteers. Went up in the morning to get an impression but it was too soon, however got this – caught that inscape in the horse that you see in the pediment especially and other basreliefs of the Parthenon and even which Sophocles had felt and expresses in two choruses of the *Oedipus Coloneus*, running on the likeness of a horse to a breaker, a wave of the sea curling over. I looked at the groin or the flank and saw how the set of the hair symmetrically flowed outwards from it to all parts of the body, so that, following that one may inscape the whole beast very simply.[116]

Here a connection is established between the thing in nature and what artists have made of it. In 1872, looking where grass has been cut in swathes on one side of a deep-set stream, Hopkins brings into sharp focus the connection between the distinctive kind of perception shown in the Journal entries above and artistic creation: he says, 'I caught an inscape as flowing and well marked almost as the frosting on glass and slabs; but I could not reproduce it afterwards with the pencil.'[117]

'I caught', in the purposeful sense which these Journal entries remind us of, dominates the meaning of 'The Windhover'. Further support for this view is given by the presence in the first tercet of the poem of 'air' meaning 'character', as in 'All the air things wear that build this world of Wales' ('In the Valley of the Elwy') and in 'As air, melody, is what strikes me most of all in music...so..."inscape" is what I above all aim at in poetry',[118] and in 'his air of angels' ('Henry Purcell'). In the octave 'air' has, of course, its other meaning – 'element we breathe' – but that rival sense is not in place in the tercet, where all the qualities mentioned actually belong to the bird itself. Hopkins 'caught' the 'air' of the falcon.

Acknowledging such a purposefulness in the poem has consequences for other lines in it, but in each case difficulties can be resolved independently as well. This is the case with 'My heart in hiding' which, it is sometimes suggested, refers to Hopkins' Jesuit life of renunciation (though it would show a very timorous view of what the religious life involved if it did). Certain of Hopkins' writings are wrongly called up in support of this biographical interpretation: he says, 'the hidden life at Nazareth is the great help to faith for us who must live more or less an obscure, constrained, and unsuccessful life' (1881);[119] in 1885 St Joseph is 'the patron of the hidden life; of those, I should think, suffering in mind and as I do',[120] and, in a letter to Dixon of 1881, St Ignatius 'lived in Rome so ordinary, so hidden a life'.[121] However, these references are to something 'hidden', not 'hiding'; and they are to a life, not a heart. If Hopkins' heart were hiding from anything in the sense the above quotations imply, it would be from public gaze, certainly not from the windhover, for the bird could not affect the obscurity which they describe.

In fact Hopkins' poem refers to the intuitive movement of something previously unresponsive. We have a sense very close to this in a letter to Bridges a little more than a year and a half after Hopkins had written 'The Windhover': 'Feeling, love in particular, is the great moving power and spring of verse and the only person that I am in love with seldom, especially now, stirs my heart sensibly.'[122] Moreover, Hopkins' use of 'heart' in his poems is very distinctive – and frequent. It is for him the primary agent in man of instinctive truth. His heart is 'Carrier-witted' ('The Wreck of the Deutschland' stanza 3); 'unteachably after evil, but uttering truth', and open also to a sort of observation, 'Ah, touched in your bower of bone, / Are you!' (stanza 18); 'My heart, but you were dovewinged' (stanza 3); or order, 'Heart, go and bleed' (stanza 31); or consultation, 'Heart, you round me right' ('Spelt from Sibyl's Leaves'); 'what sights you, heart, saw' ('I wake and feel'). 'My heart in hiding' is not a comment on Hopkins' life as a Jesuit; it is a sign that he located the capacity for emotion in the same place as anyone else would.

Those who have wished to read the poem biographically have effectively received support from others who have insisted on some dissonance between the two elements in the poem's title, for, if Christ and the windhover are in some way opposed, there must be a strong possibility that one of Christ's followers, Hopkins, is involved in the opposition. In fact there is no discord. Christ's presence, later confirmed by the 'ah my dear' quotation from George Herbert, is first allowed for by the very words which are used of the bird. The falcon is made special by the initial capital; none is warranted by usage, but a reference to God is often signalled in this way (thus, in 'The Loss of the Eurydice', line 112, we have 'Save my hero, O Hero savest'). The bird is dauphin to the kingdom of daylight: eldest son. So is Christ, Son of the Father, and possessed in Hopkins' eyes of all those knightly qualities which are associated with the bird of chivalry. The falcon's mastery of the air is Christ's, for Hopkins applauds not only the bird's achievement but the fact of the bird's existence, that there should be a thing so to master the wind, that such a thing should have been achieved (the double statement of the octave's last line). Through the windhover 'Christ our Lord' is sensed (just as Hopkins knew 'the beauty of our Lord' by that of a bluebell); the word 'chevalier' holds both Christ and the falcon together. 'A bird', 'the thing' – the general type from the world of inaccessible objects – becomes by this fusion 'my chevalier'.

However, it is not difficult to see how those who find conflict rather than fusion arrive at their position. As I have suggested above, the problem is with the final tercet. The windhover is not harmed in the poem, but the fact of Christ's martyrdom is recalled in the final image of collapsing embers: there is that major difference between them. Christ was 'doomed to succeed by failure'[123] for 'through poverty, through labour, through crucifixion his majesty of nature more shines'.[124] Christ's life in this last tercet is the paradox of the dull coal suddenly made bright in destruction; it has become an aesthetic fact as much as a moral one, and the consequences in this poem are unfortunate. Our attention is less on the crucifixion as a symbol of triumph than it is on the 'gash' of sacrifice. Yet the gash is celebrated still, and, although the mourning note of 'ah my dear' makes the celebration contained in this last tercet a quiet one, it does not cancel the fact that the crucifixion is being seen as beautiful. This seems to me regrettable.

It seems likely that 'The Windhover' will always be contested territory. Part of its fascination lies not in any special problem of the statement of the whole poem but in the fact that the 'here' which locates (and thus defines) the central event has the sort of vagueness which may accompany any ostensive gesture in print (it has only the poem's 'there' of the falcon in the air to define it by contrast). Doubtless this atmosphere of dispute does of itself give the piece distinctiveness but, apart from this, the poem is the sort of tour de force whose own existence seems to inhibit further development. Some such recognition perhaps lay behind Hopkins' saying, with years of creative work ahead of him, that it was 'the best thing I ever wrote'.[125] Both the judgement and the implicit pessimism are matters for debate.

There are but a handful of Hopkins' poems which are directly concerned with announcing that the natural world is 'charged' with God's grandeur. His 'As kingfishers catch fire' perhaps hints at the reason. Though some prefatory remarks recalling the influence of Scotus in the idea of distinctive 'selving' activity would not be out of place in a discussion of this poem, they would be secondary to the main point – might indeed obfuscate it – which is that the philosophy here so warmly held is the philosophy of a happy man. The idea that in activity a thing speaks its essential nature is at least as much a matter of mood as it is of learned intelligence. 'What I do is me: for that I came' is Hopkins' exultant proclamation about 'each mortal thing' (himself not discounted), but in Ireland he could not have said it. What he did there was manifestly not him, and such revulsion of feeling as is shown in his letters from Dublin about his life in the University stands in direct opposition to the joy so evident in this sonnet. The simple singleness of 'What I do is me' was later denied him as he tried to deal with its bitter converse and cope with a self cabined and confined. That harmony of being and doing which we have in 'As kingfishers catch fire' had left him.

The boyish playfulness of this poem ('tumbled over rim in roundy wells') and the thrill of 'Henry Purcell' are not incidental to the hold those poems have on the philosophy described in this chapter. However, there is a finality about 'The Windhover' which seems to preclude anything finer of this sort. The natural world occupied other places in Hopkins' thought than that of immediate revelation, but I pause before considering these to take up the logical issue of my discussion so far: Hopkins' attempt to fuse moral strenuousness with aesthetic inscape in the way he wrote poetry.

3

Purging the language

...poetry is emphatically speech, speech purged of dross
like gold in the furnace[1]

Words work in particular places; so generalisations about the way one
poet characteristically uses them are likely to be hazardous and not of
great value. Indeed, in such a drawing out and dismemberment his
poems are likely to die on us, and there is not much dissection in this
chapter for that reason. However, when a poet as intelligent as
Hopkins and so obviously competent in his early work in conventional
verse-forms produces so extreme a piece of experimenting as, for
example, 'Tom's Garland', we are bound to ask about the nature of
his whole poetic endeavour. We look for reassurance. It is to be found
in the achieved successes of other poems, but it is also present in the
explanations Hopkins gave in his letters and in the analyses he
presented in his notes and papers.

We should read these critically. The poetic theory they advance is
inadequate on two counts: it is not a reliable guide because the same
theory could have produced a quite different sort of poetry, and it is
unsatisfying because it does not sufficiently account for itself –
Hopkins' theory rests upon a ground of assertions which have to be
understood by going outside it. However, though the theory is not a
blueprint for his work, I see in its many facets indications of the
reasons for some of his strengths and weaknesses as a poet.

What the letters which give us Hopkins' thought do not remind us
of with sufficient force, however, is that part of Hopkins' genius
lies in the radical effort he made at detaching himself from contemporary practice. Claims about Hopkins' originality are familiar;

nonetheless, since many of the questions which his work raises relate to this very issue, it is necessary for me to make the appropriate emphasis also.

I take the opening stanza of Tennyson's 'Tithonus' as a means of throwing into relief Hopkins' own characteristic aims. The poem begins with these beautiful lines:

> The woods decay, the woods decay and fall,
> The vapours weep their burthen to the ground,
> Man comes and tills the field and lies beneath,
> And after many a summer dies the swan.

Everything here is eased by autumnal decline, for the lines are permeated by a downward movement toward rest, presented initially in the slipping off of leaves and the fall of trees. Clouds loose their weight of rain, as if in the unburdening release of tears, and man's coming and tilling is made the preliminary to rest after toil, daily sleep extended by 'beneath' into final rest. The swan's many summers are an association of the bird's grace with plenitude and fulfilment in the easy months of the year. The implied cycle is melancholy but satisfying in its sufficiency. Denied this, Tithonus, we are told, 'withers' perpetually because he is immortal, and the poem enters into its 'Ay me' mood of self-pity. The stanza closes:

> Here at the quiet limit of the world,
> A white-hair'd shadow roaming like a dream
> The ever-silent spaces of the East,
> Far-folded mists, and gleaming halls of morn.

These lines could be defended. It could be said, for example, that Tithonus' unnatural existence is being presented as shadow-like, dream-like, because it is empty of those many substantial events which give meaning to the normal, the mortal life of the opening lines. His is an existence of 'ever-silent spaces', very lonely and very pointless, his motiveless roaming contrasting with the very purposeful labour, the tilling, of the opening lines. The references to 'the quiet limit', 'the East', and 'the gleaming halls of morn' are allusions to the fact that Tithonus was loved by Eos (Aurora), the dawn goddess: they could be explained in that way. But Tennyson's earlier preference for 'vapours' instead of the more precisely locating 'clouds' should have alerted us to his propensity here to release thoughts like the drowse of incense fume. Nor is it adequate to see Tennyson's treatment of his subject as something predetermined. Tithonus here is no Struldbrug, for example, but he could have been; the 'withering' is not evoked, it is nominal (contrast Eliot's Tiresias – 'Old man with wrinkled female breasts'). The evasiveness this shows is an evasion of the definiteness which would enable us to relate Tithonus to ourselves in the ordinariness of our lives. Tennyson is using Tithonus to convey detached fine sentiment; it is thus essential that he be placed out of daily reach of man who tills the field, for in Tithonus' insubstantiality lies the reason for his existence: he is an indulgence. The sympathy we are implicitly invited to give him is pity for that larger, all-seeing consciousness (the burden of poet-consciousness) which he figures, but it is unearned; it is pity for a shadow, living not in any place or country, not in any time or any body, but in halls established only as gleams in mists which do not make one damp, cause a shiver, or block sight, but instead soften and make indiscernible the hard edges of the real.

My point here is not to argue for Hopkins' rival merits but to suggest that, surrounded as he was by poetic models such as these, the element of reaction against 'mistiness' in lines such as this one is understandable:

A cusp still clasped him, a fluke yet fanged him, ǀ entangled him, not quit
                                                                                                utterly.

Hopkins thinks of the thin crescent of moon as sticking into the dark shape of a mountain, as the fluke of an anchor would. We are given the same essential thought in three different forms and are relieved, after such repetition, when 'not quit utterly' allows us to escape from both the insistence of the sound patterns and the concentration on one idea. Nonetheless, the sharpness of the waning moon is conveyed in words which at this moment make that sharpness our essential contact with the poem-world. It is *felt* (in '*c*usp' and '*c*lasp', and 'flu*ke*' and 'fan*ged*'), not distantly observed; for this is not an Endymion's moon, diffusing appropriate sentiments; it is a hard object. In the poem from which this comes ('Moonrise') such tactility may help to provide that sense of a consciousness collecting itself on waking up by concentrating on one object of thought – this is open to debate – but we can see how precarious the success is here.

It is fancy, a *trompe-l'oeil* only, which sees the moon as sticking into the hillside, and thus the insistence on the entanglement actually comes close to whimsy. It risks producing the impression of the wrong path followed too far, followed for its own sake, followed – it could seem – out of caprice; of a misplaced emphasis that shows want of proportion in judgement and consequently makes the sound seem worked at wholly for the sake of sound, a major verbal effect in excess of the slender feeling. The hardness and realness of the words in the poem – on the tongue and ear – begin to feel separate from hardness and realness in the lived experience to which they refer.

My argument is that such separateness, where it is felt to exist, is not representative of Hopkins' merit as a poet, but that it does come from the same source as his strengths. Preoccupied with form and strictness, he resisted the contemporary tendency to lengthy and formless effusiveness, applying his idea of 'inscape' to poetry and turning with affection to the exacting models of Welsh bards. He coupled with his interest in form an emphasis on poetry as a spoken thing, using the language of heard speech; but there is a conflict of interests between the two that Hopkins did not sufficiently recognise, and it is to this failure – a failure connected with the precarious isolation in which Hopkins had put himself – that I attribute what may appear superficially to be verbal eccentricity in him. I see as the main trend in his work the selective employment of the resources of the English language so as to develop in his verse the rigour which characterised his spiritual life. Although this chapter has many component parts, this is its main theme.

Hopkins' methods of composition owe more to the bard than the scribe, but since it is easy to suppose, in view of the sheer difficulty of some of his technical demands, that the reverse is true, some description of these methods is necessary to readjust the picture his letters sometimes seem to give of a mere technician at work. Hopkins did not coldly type-set the syllables of his poems. He believed early that 'one cannot reach Parnassus except by flying thither',[2] and a critical Patmore, quoting Milton, passed on the fact that Hopkins 'assures me that "his thoughts involuntary moved" in such numbers, and that he did not write them from preconceived theories'.[3] The glimpses we have from the letters of Hopkins at work often corroborate the claimed spontaneity. 'Hurrahing in Harvest' was 'the outcome of half an hour of extreme enthusiasm as I walked home alone one day from fishing in the Elwy',[4] 'Spring and Fall' was composed 'walking from Lydiate',[5] four sonnets of desolation came 'like inspirations unbidden and against my will',[6] and even 'St. Alphonsus Rodriguez', 'written to order' in celebration of the canonisation of the Society's lay brother, 'was made out of doors in the Phoenix Park with my mind's eye on the first presentment of the thought'.[7] It is true that this picture is complicated by the fact that work not completed in the first 'jet of inspiration'[8] might often be allowed to lie 'soaking'[9] or be touched up[10] in its details, sometimes over a number of years, and that sometimes he tried to manage by forced labour when inspiration failed him (from Oxford he writes that he is seldom stirred now: 'Then again I have of myself made verse so laborious';[11] from Glasgow, that the vein of poetry soon dried in the city, 'and I do not know if I can coax it to run again...I am sometimes surprised at myself how slow and laborious a thing verse is to me'[12]), but, in general, work not finished would have to wait until Hopkins' creative vein was flowing again or, more frequently and to his bitter regret, go forever uncompleted. We must suppose that a piece as long as 'The Wreck of the Deutschland' was composed at the desk, but the bulk of Hopkins' poetry is in varieties of the Petrarchan sonnet form (sometimes lengthened by the addition of codas, sometimes shortened as a 'curtal' sonnet), and some at least of his sonnets he composed in his head. Thus from Ireland he tells Patmore 'such verse as I do compose is oral, made away from paper, and I put it down with repugnance',[13] which suits with the picture given to Bridges from Glasgow: 'One night...I had some glowing thoughts and lines, but I did not put them down and I fear they may fade to little or nothing.'[14] He usually thinks of himself as 'making'[15] a poem rather than writing one, an emphasis which, in context, suggests the independent life of the completed work.

Given, then, that in Hopkins we have a poet whose work is as much dependent on the unbidden, the inspired, as that of any other creative artist, how shall we account for the legislative effort, the talk of 'rules' and 'laws' and 'strictness', which permeates his letters to his poet friends? It was, F. R. Leavis shrewdly observes (of the technical Author's Preface which Hopkins wrote for Bridges' MS book of his poems), 'his way of strengthening his hold on his creative impulses and perceptions and justifying to himself as far as possible, in terms of his training, he being a contemporary of Bridges, his scandalous experiments'.[16] One can readily see Hopkins' need to fortify himself by giving to his position of lonely dissent the force of law, and Dr Leavis' judgement may be extended to cover Hopkins' other announcements of what he was about. Hopkins' poetic theory was his way of relating to a norm when his own poetry was so obviously at odds with any norm then current. It was his means of reaching behind contemporary poetry – the poetry of Swinburne, Tennyson, and the rondeliers – in attempting to give himself definition with relation to officially great poetry, that of Milton and Shakespeare. We should be foolish to accept uncritically his own estimations (obviously his verse is not Miltonic, and his claimed affinity with Dryden is best judged as a statement of allegiance – for example, it separates him from Arnold, who thought Dryden no poet, for reasons I give later in this chapter), but we should see it as part of Hopkins' achievement that he recognised the need for a change of direction in English poetry and, in part, what that change should involve.

Hopkins had his eyes set on the future as the only place outside heaven which would vindicate his belief that what was currently popular was in fact ephemeral: 'You think, as I do,' he wrote to Patmore, 'that our modern poets are too voluminous: time will mend this, their volumes will sink.'[17] Aghast at 'all that wildness of words which one is lost in in every copy of magazine verses one comes across',[18] he had evolved a sort of poetry – and a theory to support it – which was in one dimension a critique of contemporary practice. Was verse currently prolix? – the merit of a poem may well lie 'in its terseness'.[19] Was it sprawling and formless? – 'design'[20] he aims at above all else. Did it seek spurious dignity by employing old-fashioned words? – archaism was a 'blight', the language of poetry should be the current one.[21] Would readers find him *so* different, if he tried to publish, as to dismiss him as odd? – to justify himself in his isolation (this seems to me the chief explanation for his stress on uniqueness) he countered with a heavy emphasis on individuality grounded, as it were, in natural law: 'each poet is like a species in nature...and can never recur'.[22]

If his hostility is revealing, so is his praise. In my first chapter I suggested an opposition in Hopkins of energy, rigour, abnegation, against luxury, indulgence, passivity. This is reflected in the approval of manliness he gives when supporting other poets: Bridges' sonnets are 'full of manly tenderness',[23] they are 'marked with character throughout',[24] whereas 'the Swinburnian kind' of poetry 'expresses passion but not feeling, much less character'.[25] That sort is 'crying always in a high head voice about flesh and flowers and democracy and damnation'.[26] 'In point of character, of sincerity or earnestness, of manliness, of tenderness' Bridges has what Tennyson, Swinburne, and Morris have not got 'and seem scarcely to think worth having';[27] he is 'manly and tender'.[28] This is praise beyond the gratuities that might anyway be expected of friendship, but the qualities are not unique to his friend: Aeschylus too had 'earnestness of spirit and would-be piety', 'touching consideration', and 'manly tenderness'[29] (again the important qualifying 'manly'). Dryden is 'the most masculine of our poets';[30] in contrast the villanelle is 'an effeminate thing: I wish we were rid of them'.[31] (It is not immediately important that history has overturned some of these judgements; their present significance lies in the criteria Hopkins employs in making them.) So too Hopkins laments the death of Elizabethan English, of 'the living masculine native rhetoric of that age'.[32] Thus in Hopkins' statements about his own work we should expect some claim to a similar kind of masculine strength.

In fact we have something more complicated. His claim for one poem that it will be 'severe, no experiments'[33] is both a sign of the expected masculine rigour and an acknowledgement that it is sometimes missing. How comes this contradiction?

It issues from a fundamental difficulty in Hopkins' poetic that – in theoretic terms – he never resolved or even admitted. 'Every true poet', he thought, 'must be original and originality a condition of poetic genius',[34] and he regretted that one Irish poet whom he had read lacked the one enduring essential which is effectively the guarantee of originality, in short '*inscape*, that is species or individually-distinctive beauty of style'.[35] In the word lies the difficulty. Inasmuch as it means 'individually-distinctive' it is expressive of the uniqueness of the artist – he is doing something which has not been done before. However, poetry is also 'speech...employed to carry the inscape of speech for the inscape's sake',[36] and that is something different.

The difference is obscured because Hopkins has used the same term in relation to both functions, but when he refers to individual distinctiveness he is speaking of the need for the artist to be different from those who have preceded him, to be true to his 'self'; when he speaks of 'the inscape of speech' he is concerned with the duty of art to share in the larger life outside it, its duty not to be narrowly literary in what he called the 'cultshah'[37] manner. Of course, the two roles are not incompatible – every great poet's verse is a private working of the public medium of language – but there are problems created by Hopkins' use of 'inscape' to apply to both. The inscape of speech – its very soul, its essential self – obviously cannot be the essential distinctiveness of an artist's work. How are the two claims to be reconciled when the inscape of speech must be that which great poets have in common and their own inscapes the things which distinguish them? Furthermore, Hopkins seems to have been uncertain about whether inscape (of either sort) was something achieved anyway in the course of writing well, as his idea of a poet being a species in nature suggests, or whether it was something deliberate, as his '"inscape" is what I above all aim at in poetry'[38] suggests.

Hopkins formulated principles relating to the craftsmanship of poetry which he plainly regarded as applicable to people other than himself, and at the same time he was at work on verse for which no theory could adequately account because it was uniquely his own. In Ireland he said of one piece that 'It is in a commoner and smoother style than I mostly write in, but that is no harm: I am sure I have gone far enough in oddities',[39] but this did not stop him producing his most extreme experiment ('Tom's Garland') hardly more than six months later. His experiments were of course investigations into what is possible with English, not self-congratulatory ingenuities. Thus, in the first-offered draft of 'St. Alphonsus Rodriguez', we have this:

> Yet God the mountain-mason, continent-
> Quarrier, earthwright;

with its characteristic Hopkinsian devices, here used unsuccessfully – marked alliteration, triplicated phrasing ('earthwright' would suffice on its own), imagery which is – here – a list rather than a development. But Hopkins senses the objections, for he says, 'Or, against singularity, we may try this',[40] and removes the weaknesses in two alternatives which come much closer to the final and superb

> Yet God (that hews mountain and continent,
> Earth, all, out;

where the earth-sculpting is not merely mentioned but is made active in 'hews...out'. 'Against singularity', 'what I want...to be... less singular, is an audience';[41] but singularity, according to one of the facets of Hopkins' theory, was what he should have been cultivating.

In general, we see Hopkins' singularity (our sense of his faults is very much a question of what we *see*; his singularity exists also in successes which, because they are that, pass notice) whenever he allows sound to enfeeble sense, and this is true whenever sound appears to exist for its own sake so that the semantic core of a word has been lost and we are left dealing with the husk. Thus the assonantal interest which Dr Leavis so rightly locates as one of Hopkins' strengths[42] can nonetheless result in such a case. In 'Stigma, signal cinquefoil token' ('The Wreck of the Deutschland', stanza 22) the words have become pieces of sound, their physical presence in the mouth so powerfully felt in the patterns of alliteration, assonance, and consonance which 'stig', 'sig', and 'cinq', and 'ma', 'na', and 'ue' make, that the important need for words to be different sounds if they are to represent different meanings has gone unacknowledged; the delicate relation between the concreteness of the spoken sound and the abstractness of that for which it stands has been seriously damaged. This kind of submergence of sound-identities in general patterns is observable elsewhere in Hopkins.

Lists are tedious, but one further example will perhaps clarify my meaning: 'wears, bears, cares and combs' ('To R. B.') takes up the attention of the mind with similarities when development of thought requires that differences should be marked.

There are occasions in Hopkins' poems when sound-patterns have so determined the selection of words that that other quality of language, its ability to work by association, has been disregarded. Thus, in 'The Bugler's First Communion', the boy's father is described with unwitting grotesqueness as 'an English sire'. It is regrettable that such a grossness should result from Hopkins' attempt to avoid monotonously obvious patterns by carrying over the completion of a rhyme into the following line's initial letter: hence, here, 'Irish...sire (he/Sh)'. When the lines are spoken with the pause that sense demands the effect is buried deep in the fabric of the poem; when pointed out the phonic subtlety looks as gross to the eye as the semantic ugliness to which on this occasion it has given rise (read so as to bring out the rhyme which Hopkins has been at pains to conceal, it would sound grosser still). He used the same effect frequently in 'The Loss of the Eurydice' ('wrecked her? he/C... electric', lines 23–4; 'coast or/M...snowstorm', lines 67–8), and in 'Hurrahing in Harvest' only study would bring out 'Saviour ...gave you a/R'. In 'The Candle Indoors' we are given this sound-pattern: 'Or to-fro tender trambeams truckle at the eye'. The trinket effect of all those dentals is at odds with the trundling bulk of 'tram' and of 'beam' which, anxious though one may be to make it refer to a ray of light, suffers in association. The guidance that 'tram' may mean 'silk thread'[43] does not help one to resolve that initial impression into an effective description of the play of light upon the eye. The reader must then react adversely to the line, or else make a willed attempt to shed the associations which his non-poetic experience of language has given him and share the privacy of Hopkins' more recondite phrase.

'His manner', said Yeats, was 'a last development of poetical diction.'[44] It was not; but this charge carries most force when it is applied to lines such as the one just quoted from 'The Candle Indoors'. However, it should not be allowed to stand, because it encourages the notion that Hopkins was wilfully esoteric and that one should treasure him for this (or else reject the whole corpus of his work). It is arguable that any reading of poetry involves clarification in the reader's understanding and hence the shedding of false impressions, but this is not the same as denying any ordinary experience of language. Hopkins failed lamentably on one or two occasions to make himself understood, and those occasions do not become less lamentable when his letters provide the necessary gloss. We have such a case with 'sakes' in the ugly 'only I'll/Have an eye to the sakes of him', from 'Henry Purcell'. Hopkins said of 'sake', 'I mean by it the being a thing has outside itself, as a voice by its echo, a face by its reflection, a body by its shadow, a man by his name, fame, or memory',[45] but knowing this does not improve the poetry. *We* mean by 'sake' 'important cause' or 'serious advantage' and accordingly we use it in the singular, so that Hopkins' 'sakes' has a cancelling effect; it is as if someone were saying 'his souls'. Moreover, 'sake' is more important to us – we say 'for the child's sake', 'for His name's sake' – than an echo or a shadow. Hopkins himself knew that 'sakes' was 'hazardous' and that his own creativeness was at odds with understanding here.[46]

He could, of course, use the obscure word successfully, but, where he does, it has often, in Eliot's way, begun to communicate before it is properly understood. Such a word is 'sloggering' in 'the rash smart sloggering brine' of 'The Wreck of the Deutschland'. It means, Professor MacKenzie points out, 'the action of a prize-fighter raining blows on his opponent; behind it lies the dialect "slog: to strike with great force"'.[47] Something of its meaning might, in fact, be deduced from its poetic context.

My suggestion, then, is that in the ambiguous theory of 'inscape' Hopkins had not only developed a means of justifying his own uniqueness but also burdened himself with an idea according to which mere novelty might be valued just because it was new; instead of trusting to his originality to show itself he was tempted to seek an entirely spurious distinctiveness, to become mannered. He recognised the risk, anticipating opposition to 'Tom's Garland' and 'Harry Ploughman' by saying that they were 'works of infinite, of over great contrivance, I am afraid, to the annulling in the end of the right effect',[48] and he conceded his need for readers. But readers of what sort? Readers with expectations nurtured on Tennyson and Swinburne? Some of the responsibility for the weaknesses we find in Hopkins' work rests with the fact that the traditions of poetry then current obliged him to rely too heavily on his own isolated judgement.

Their cause has been located elsewhere (and the faults have been seen as representative of the whole): 'It is the Keatsian luxury carried one stage further, luxuriating in the kinetic and muscular.'[49] This appears to suit well with what I have said above about the physical presence of the words in the mouth, but 'luxury' suggests, pejoratively, a sort of sensuous abandonment which I consider to be the reverse of the truth. It is not the presence in Hopkins of 'the kinetic and muscular' which is in dispute, then, but the question of whether Hopkins' use of them was self-indulgent (self-indulgence in effort is unusual, but the charge is not on that ground to be rejected). Whether Hopkins' strength was of that self-interested kind, or whether it was supple and serviceable, is a matter which will become clear only in discussion of individual poems (I maintain it was, but I certainly have no wish to defend against the charge that Hopkins' language was 'muscle-bound'[50] the disjunctions of 'Tom's Garland', the clotted sounds of 'Harry Ploughman', or the strains of 'Henry Purcell'). However, the implication that 'Keatsian luxury' operated more generally in Hopkins needs to be resisted here.

The accusation of 'luxury' is a reapplication of one of Hopkins' own critical judgements. He qualified his view that the youthful Keats was fit to be set beside the youthful Shakespeare[51] when, on rereading him, he came to feel that Keats' verse was at every turn 'abandoning itself to an unmanly and enervating luxury'. 'His mind', said Hopkins, 'had...the distinctively masculine powers in abundance, his character the manly virtues, but while he gave himself up to dreaming and self indulgence of course they were in abeyance.'[52] The judgement is interesting in the present context because it bears on Hopkins' own case. With his attention on the earlier work Dr Leavis says of Hopkins that he had 'in an age pervaded by Keatsian aspirations...the essential Keatsian strength'. He then qualifies the judgement in a way that many who have shared it have not: 'The mature work...doesn't prompt us with Keats's name so obviously.'[53] The reason is that the Keatsian strength is now allied with Hopkinsian stringency. 'Ooze of oil' issues not into sensations for mouth or for fingers but into 'Crushed'; 'warm breast' is given over immediately to 'bright wings'; the tenderness of the 'pushed peach' to which Hopkins likens his Boy Bugler's easy acceptance receives, again, no further evocation. Thus any imputation of sensuous luxury underlying the idea 'Keatsian luxury carried one stage further' should be rejected. Presented with a poetry which has in it lines such as (from 'Duns Scotus's Oxford')

> Thou hast a base and brickish skirt there, sours
> That neighbour-nature thy grey beauty is grounded
> Best in

'luxury' is not a word which comes easily to mind: this poetry is, if anything, too severe – we do not readily tolerate Hopkins' omission of the softening 'which' in the first line, nor, on this occasion, his moving 'Best in' to a place where the heaviest metrical weight will fall on the plosive. Given such lines, Dr Leavis' reference – partly an ironic one – to 'consonantal "harshness"'[54] is seen as well placed.

Such severity is allowed for by Hopkins' theory because he thought of one of his aims in terms of a metaphor whose meaning he could interpret at will. Despite an occasional reference claiming wider scope for it, it is clear from his Journal usages that 'inscape' relates to seeing. Thus to refer to 'inscape of speech' is to use the term figuratively and to do something akin to what Shakespeare was doing when he had Hamlet say that drama's aim was 'to hold...the mirror up to nature': mirrors are dumb and may be turned at will in the hands of their users; they do not present five-act plays in blank verse. 'Inscape of speech' is a metaphor involving a shift in the senses similar to that involved in Hopkins' reference to poetry as a 'shape'[55] of speech. These are usages which can mean virtually what one wishes. The figurativeness in his thinking is plain too when he writes of 'the naked thew and sinew of the English language',[56] or asks,

Is it free from the taint of Elizabethan English? Does it not stink of that? for the sweetest flesh turns to corruption. Is not Elizabethan English a corpse these centuries?[57]

(Though these last two observations with their predications of strength and life are more clearly defining.) If 'inscape' or 'shape' of speech is metaphorical, what did Hopkins understand by it?

We are shown in one of those elliptical statements of his which effectively say something nearly the contrary of what, at first sight, they seem to be so firmly announcing: 'the poetical language of an age shd. be the current language heightened, to any degree heightened and unlike itself'.[58] What a qualification – a language 'unlike itself'! How Hopkins came to it may perhaps be made clearer in contrast with the view Matthew Arnold would advance in print the following year (1880), for each was struggling with the problem of what makes poetry special.

The focal point of the conflict is the question of language, particularly as it touches the Augustans. In a dialogue which Hopkins wrote, 'On the Origin of Beauty', he had said that 'Dryden...seems to take thoughts that are not by nature poetical...but under a kind of living force like fire they are powerfully changed and incandescent.'[59] Twenty-two years later he was still praising him.[60] For Arnold, however, Dryden is no poet but a classic of our prose.[61] Hopkins was indignant at that view: not to think Dryden a poet was one of 'the loutish falls and hideous vagaries of the human mind'.[62] But it was entirely consistent of Arnold to dismiss Dryden as he did. Poetry, the poetry which will one day replace 'most of what now passes with us for religion and philosophy',[63] had to have the loftiest of spiritual homes if it was to make good this claim. It had to come from the soul, a soul seemingly not the seat of intelligence; it had to be extraordinary, had to be remote from prose. Now in Dryden's time, 'A fit prose was a necessity; but it was impossible that a fit prose should establish itself amongst us without some touch of frost to the imaginative life of the soul.'[64] For Arnold the interests of prose and those of verse are antithetic and it is this antithesis which is behind his indictment of Pope and Dryden:

The needful qualities for a fit prose are regularity, uniformity, precision, balance...But an almost exclusive attention to these qualities involves some repression and silencing of poetry.[65]

It was because Thomas Gray was born in an age when such attention was the norm that his own production was so scanty: he was unlucky. Nonetheless Gray was a poet and Dryden was not and – most tellingly, when one bears Hopkins' ideas in mind – Arnold quotes with approval Gray's observations on poetry:

'As to matter of style, I have this to say: The language of the age is never the language of poetry;...Our poetry...has a language peculiar to itself, to which almost every one that has written has added something.'[66]

What does Arnold think of this? 'It is impossible for a poet to lay down the rules of his own art with more insight, soundness, and certainty.'[67] Writing in his Preface to *Poems* (1853) he says that those who look to the classics to provide them with models are 'more truly than others under the empire of facts, and more independent of the language current among those with whom they live'.[68] For Arnold, then, 'the language of the age is never the language of poetry', the two are necessarily separate; for Hopkins, first and foremost 'the poetical language of an age shd. be the current language'.

Arnold thus has poetry recoiling from the everyday prose world (the world of his Hebraisers) in order to establish its identity by specialism and exclusiveness. Hopkins, however, though resisting this, has yet to distinguish verse from prose. He seems open to the objections which Coleridge advanced against Wordsworth's 'language really used by men' (that, for example, men do not speak poetry), but both this and the further potential challenge – whose current language: Sam Weller's or Cardinal Newman's? (Wordsworth seemed to have resolved that question) – are circumvented by Hopkins' insistence on 'heightening' so that the current language may become 'unlike itself'. The current language is the language spoken by Hopkins; his 'heightening' involves dispensing with what might be regarded as inessentials, notably slack syllables which are present only to fulfil the requirements of metre and which appear to carry little meaning (such syllables are often, grammatically, relatives). It also involves a concentration of the sound-resources of the language with the aim of power rather than, for example, of grace. Such a selectiveness as this – a reaction against mere decorousness – may fairly be called what Hopkins called it, a purging. The rest of this chapter is about the means by which he carried it out.

The language Hopkins thought of himself as purging to its essentials, as if to arrive at the condition of Milton's poetry or Purcell's music, which are 'something necessary and eternal',[69] was spoken language. This has so many implications for his practice that it is worth quoting at length from a recently published letter to his brother Everard which gives his view in developed form:

> Poetry was originally meant for either singing or reciting; a record was kept of it; the record could be, was, read, and that in time by one reader, alone, to himself, with the eyes only. This reacted on the art: what was to be performed under these conditions[,] for these conditions ought to be and was composed and calculated. Sound-effects were intended, wonderful combinations even; but they bear the marks of having been meant for the whispered, not even whispered, merely mental performance of the closet, the study and so on. You follow, Edward Joseph? You do: then we are there. This is not the true nature of poetry, the darling child of lips and spoken utterance: it must be spoken; *till it is spoken it is not performed*, it does not perform, it is not itself. Sprung rhythm gives back to poetry its true soul and self. As poetry is emphatically speech, speech purged of dross like gold in the furnace, so it must have emphatically the essential elements of speech. Now emphasis itself, stress, is one of these: sprung rhythm makes verse stressy; it purges it to an emphasis as much brighter, livelier, more lustrous than the regular but commonplace emphasis of common rhythm as poetry in general is brighter than common speech.[70]

Sprung rhythm I treat in a moment, but I should like to take up here Hopkins' 'this reacted on the art'. The way *he* conceived poetry reacted on *his* art. When one comes to Hopkins for the first time the difficulty one might have with any new poet – the difficulty of determining in an elementary way what is going on – seems in Hopkins' case to be too predominantly a syntactical business. (Hence the mistaken judgement that Hopkins says simple things in a difficult way.) In fact, much of the exasperation which some people experience with Hopkins on first meeting is due to a radical confusion of modes: they are expecting a message, he has provided something more in the nature of a musical score. The typographic message is silent and cerebral, immediate and physically self-sufficient; the score awaits implementation, is an anticipation of sound to come, is unsatisfyingly incomplete. Moreover, grammar is the elaborate controlling convention by which the silent message is made accessible to the reader, but heard speech is often ungrammatical.[71] Sentences may be broken off at will, phrases amplified to the point where they usurp the place of the main structure, and the sigh or the gasp becomes rich with meaning. In spoken language intonation is more important than grammar, and becomes the ultimate control-system by which meaning is achieved. Many of the superficial problems connected with Hopkins are attendant on this shift (it is, of course, to mistake the nature of his endeavour to say that he was writing for readers and should have observed the conventions).

He himself seems to have realised only slowly the fundamental change he was requiring in a reader's attitude. His first instruction puts the reader in the role of listener not performer: read ('The Loss of the Eurydice') 'with your ears, as if the paper were declaiming it at you'.[72] A year later this has become more physical: 'take breath and read it with the ears'.[73] Three years after that (1882) 'read it aloud',[74] but only in Ireland do we get to the point reached in the letter cited above and repeated to Bridges: 'it is, as living art should be, made for performance'.[75] His manuscripts were notations, 'writing as the record of speech',[76] a way of transmitting the real poem but not the thing itself.

The speaking voice can afford to pay less regard to grammar, for it resolves difficulties by way of intonation; the tape-recorder would have given Hopkins a useful aid. However, it is doubtful if it would necessarily have improved his poetry. Intonation resolves difficulties that typographical reproduction proliferates, but intonation does not produce eloquence. The difference between the spoken and the written word may fairly explain some of the risks Hopkins took with syntax, but it may not always be fairly entered as a plea in mitigation. I give some examples. Firstly, from 'Henry Purcell', 'So some great stormfowl. . .fans fresh our wits with wonder,' is not difficult to comprehend; but insert

> whenever he has walked his while
> The thunder-purple seabeach plumèd purple-of-thunder,
> If a wuthering of his palmy snow-pinions scatter a colossal smile
> Off him, but meaning motion

and we have a sentence of inordinate length and complexity. 'It is just the same when some great stormfowl with thunder-purple feathers, strutting in his time along a thunder-purple beach, then beats his snowy wings like the spreading of a great smile and, intent only on motion, nonetheless fans our wits fresh with wonder': subject and predicate are so estranged in time that it is hard for the mind to hold them together. Intonation can only bring out what is there to be demonstrated: in the first lines of the same poem ('Have fair fallen, O fair, fair have fallen, so dear / To me, so arch-especial a spirit as heaves in Henry Purcell') 'fallen' does not mean 'befallen', the meaning Hopkins intended us to grasp.[77] As it stands it needs a preposition, '*to* so dear / To me'; the connection between the verb and the object is missing entirely. So, too, in 'Tom's Garland', in 'Commonweal / Little Í reck ho! lacklevel in, if all had bread', there is no relation to be uncovered between little recking the Common-weal and 'lacklevel', It 'is all very well for those who are in, however low in, the Commonwealth',[78] says Hopkins' gloss, but 'those who' is missing in the poem; the only subjects at this point are 'I' and 'all'. This piece is so obviously in some of its parts a series of semantic lurches that it is needless to rehearse all the lacunae in it – that, for example, 'no way sped' has no subject, and that 'gold go garlanded / With, perilous, O no,' is similarly deprived, 'perilous' floating around without possibility of connection: Hopkins has left out too much.

In general that is not true of his work; he achieved the particular intensification, the 'heightening', which he sought. He was aided in this by the full employment in perhaps something over half his completed poems, and by the partial use in others, of the regular irregularity of sprung rhythm. He used it in pieces as different as the quiet lyric 'Spring and Fall' and the weighty and sombre 'Spelt from Sibyl's Leaves', so it was not the determining factor in his art, nor, in view of his successes in standard rhythm, was it indispensable to him. However, Hopkins made much of it, and for sound reasons. He explained why to Bridges:

Why do I employ sprung rhythm at all? Because it is the nearest to the rhythm of prose, that is the native and natural rhythm of speech, the least forced, the most rhetorical and emphatic of all possible rhythms, combining, as it seems to me, opposite, and one wd. have thought, incompatible excellences, markedness of rhythm – that is rhythm's self – and naturalness of expression – for why, if it is forcible in prose to say 'lashed : rod', am I obliged to weaken this in verse, which ought to be stronger, not weaker, into 'láshed birch-ród' or something?[79]

Emphasis and strength (conceived of primarily in terms of emphasis) are the chief objectives here; 'naturalness of expression' is made possible by the freer disposition of stresses within a line, but is a secondary advantage as Hopkins describes sprung rhythm in this passage: he is preoccupied with what is 'forcible'. The principle of sprung rhythm is lucidly described in letters to Dixon: 'To speak shortly, it consists in scanning by accents or stresses alone, without any account of the number of syllables, so that a foot may be one strong syllable or it may be many light and one strong';[80] 'the word Sprung which I use for this rhythm means something like *abrupt* and applies by rights only where one stress follows another running, without syllable between'.[81] The history of Hopkins' development of this idea once more gives support to the idea of a gradual evolution in him, uninterrupted by his joining the Jesuits.

When Hopkins wrote to Dixon in 1878 about the composition of 'The Wreck of the Deuschland' he told him, 'I had long had haunting my ear the echo of a new rhythm which I now realised on paper.'[82] The 'new rhythm' had in fact haunted his ear for seven years; his first attempt in it was not 'The Wreck of the Deutschland' but the experimental 'Lines for a Picture of St. Dorothea', a reworking of his earlier 'For a Picture of St. Dorothea' (1864) and the last poem he sent to Bridges before he became a Jesuit. We have seen that, strictly, sprung rhythm is characterised by two stresses following in sequence with no intervening slack syllable. Individual lines in the St Dorothea poem have this feature (the stress marks are Hopkins' own):

> I' am so' light' and fair'
> Quínces, look', when' not one'
> But' they came' from' the south'
> Which' is it', star' or dew'?

However, the conclusive evidence lies in the continuity between the examples used in Hopkins' postscript to Bridges and those he subsequently used to explain sprung rhythm:

P.S. I hope you will master the peculiar beat I have introduced into St Dorothea. The development is mine but the beat is in Shakespeare – e.g.

> Whý should thís desert be? – and

> Thoú for whóm Jóve would swear – where the rest of the

lines are eight-syllabled or seven-syllabled.[83]

The same examples occur in Hopkins' lecture-notes entitled

'Rhythm and the other structural parts of Rhetoric – verse' (1873–4).
The relevant section reads:

This beat-rhythm allows of development as much as time-rhythm whenever the
ear or mind is true enough to take in the essential principle of it, that beat is
measured by stress or strength, not number, so that one strong may be equal not
only to two weak but to less or more. In English great masters of rhythm have
acted on this:
 Shakespeare –

                    Toád that uńder cóld stóne
             and –
                    Sleép thou fírst i'th chármed pót
             and –
                    Why should thís désert bé?
             and –
                    Thoú for whóm Jóve would swéar – [84]

'The peculiar beat' has now become 'this beat-rhythm' but the
illustrations used are identical. In 1877 'this beat-rhythm' has a
name, and Hopkins' reference to 'lecturing' seems to point back to
his notes of 1873–4:

I do not of course claim to have invented *sprung rhythms* but only *sprung rhythm*;
I mean that single lines and single instances of it are not uncommon in English
and I have pointed them out in lecturing – e.g. 'why should this : desert be?'[85]

(The list of examples which follows includes Campbell's 'as ye
sweep:through the deep', which also occurs in the 1873–4 lecture-
notes.) We thus have clear evidence of continuity in Hopkins'
thought on prosody: what is in its formative stages in 1868 is to be
seen as an acknowledged principle in 1873–4 and established
poetically in 1875–6 in 'The Wreck of the Deutschland'.

Hopkins later realised that sprung rhythm 'existed in full force in
Anglo saxon verse'[86] and that his achievement was not to have
invented it but to have revived it, independently of older influence,
for modern poetry. In fact, what he had produced was something
more sophisticated than what had existed before. The limits of the
previous system are indicated by W. K. Wimsatt and Monroe C.
Beardsley in an essay on English metre in which they say of 'the
very old (and recently revived) meter of strong stress' that 'the
gabble of weaker syllables, now more, now fewer, between the major
stresses obscures all the minor stresses and relieves them of any
structural duty',[87] and further observe,

One of the disadvantages of the old strong-stress meter is doubtless its limited capacity for interplay. The stress pattern of the meter is so nearly the same as the stress pattern of the syntax and logic that there is nothing much for the meter to interplay with...Where such meters gain in freedom and direct speech-feeling, they lose in opportunity for precise interplay.[88]

Thus they say of Eliot's deployment of both the strong-stress and regular-stress systems within the same stanza, 'This is playing in and out of the metrical inheritance.'[89] What Hopkins seems to have done, in contrast, was to attempt a combination of the two systems. He said as much of some of his sonnets,[90] and such a combination is evident elsewhere - in 'The Wreck of the Deutschland', for example, of which this is the fifth stanza (my stress-marks):

> I am sóft síft
> In an hóurglass – át the wáll
> Fást, but míned with a mótion, a dríft,
> And it crówds and it cómbs to the fáll;
> I stéady as a wáter in a wéll, to a póise, to a páne,
> But róped with, álways, áll the way dówn from the táll
> Félls or flánks of the vóel, a véin
> Of the góspel próffer, a préssure, a prínciple, Chríst's gíft.

In lines 4 and 5 here a regular anapaestic pattern emerges, but this does no violence to the principle of sprung rhythm that one stress makes one foot, even if the number of attached slack syllables is the same for a number of feet running. Such a return seems to be a tacit acknowledgement of the point which Wimsatt and Beardsley make about the stress-metre's limited capacity for interplay; it may also account for Hopkins' saying that the great variety of sprung rhythm 'amounts to a counterpointing' when he knew full well that the sort of rhythmic expectation which is necessary to counterpoint is outside the scope of what is in essence – as far as stress considerations alone are concerned – an irregular system.[91]

There is an additional reason for suggesting that sprung rhythm is, in part at least, an attempt to combine rather than juxtapose the merits of strong-stress and regular-stress systems: it aims at a sort of regularity, and this by taking account not simply of weight but also of time. To deal with the core of the theory, namely the possibility that two stressed syllables occur together, with no slack syllable between: what happens on such occasions is that the voice, instead of as it were treading lightly on an intermediate unstressed syllable, pauses briefly between the two stresses. This is how we avoid turning 'lashed rod' into 'lashtrod'. Hopkins described stressing a syllable as 'making...more' of it.[92] This may involve saying one syllable more loudly than another; it will in any case involve taking longer over saying it than over saying nearby unstressed syllables. Thus, in the system of diacritical marks which Hopkins developed for his poems over the years and which we see at its most complex in the 'Harry Ploughman' MS, we have:

marks used:
(1) ∧ strong stress; which does not differ much from
(2) ⌢ pause or dwell on a syllable, which need not however have the metrical stress

How the two marks differ at all Hopkins does not say (he may have had loudness in mind). His list continues:

(3) ´ the metrical stress, marked in doubtful cases only;
(4) ∼ quiver or circumflexion, making one syllable nearly two, most used with diphthongs and liquids;
(5) ⌢ between syllables slurs them into one;
(6) ‿ over three or more syllables gives them the time of one half foot
(7) ∪ the outride; under one or more syllables makes them extrametrical: a slight pause follows as if the voice were silently making its way back to the highroad of the verse.[93]

Excepting the first and third, all these marks obviously involve timing; my suggestion is that even the apparent exceptions do as well.

The timing does not aim at producing feet which are equal on that basis alone, but it is part of an attempt at equality. Hopkins tells Bridges that 'Since the syllables in sprung rhythm are not counted, time or equality in strength is of more importance than in common counted rhythm',[94] and affirms to Dixon that this sense of equality is what makes the difference between 'its εἶναι and its εὖ εἶναι, the writing it somehow and the writing it as it should be written'.[95] Then Hopkins tries to explain:

We must distinguish strength (or gravity) and length. About length there is little difficulty: plainly *bidst* is longer than *bids* and *bids* than *bid*. But it is not recognized by everybody that *bid*, with a flat dental, is graver or stronger than *bit*, with a sharp. The strongest and, other things being alike, the longest syllables are those with the circumflex, like *fire*. Any syllable ending in *ng*, though *ng* is only a single sound, may be made as long as you like by prolonging the nasal. So too *n* may be prolonged after a long vowel or before a consonant, as in *soon* or *and*... I have put these down at random as samples.[96]

Hopkins sets out to make a distinction between his two ways of achieving equality ('strength' and time) and ends up instead by conflating the two: 'the strongest *and* [my italics]...the longest syllables are those...like *fire*'. The same conjunction occurs in his Author's Preface: 'In Sprung Rhythm...the feet are assumed to be equally long or strong and their seeming inequality is made up by pause or stressing.'[97] This dual formula is repeated in the claim for one poem (probably 'The Leaden Echo and the Golden Echo') that 'everything is weighed and timed'.[98] But how shall we measure the weight and how judge the time when some syllables may be made 'as long as you like'? It is not surprising that Hopkins evolved such an elaborate set of marks as those to be found on the 'Harry Ploughman' MS: he was trying to control time. As if he had taken Pater's figure literally, his art really does begin, in the poet's judgement, to approach the condition of music. 'Thou art indeed just, Lord' 'must be read *adagio molto* and with great stress',[99] and 'Spelt from Sibyl's Leaves' should be performed with

loud, leisurely, poetical (not rhetorical) recitation, with long rests, long dwells on the rhyme and other marked syllables, and so on. This sonnet shd. be almost sung: it is most carefully timed in *tempo rubato*.[100]

This sonnet 'essays effects almost musical'.[101] Indeed, 'by a consideration of what the music of the verse requires', says Hopkins, one may sometimes recover lost pronunciations (so, he says, 'heavy' must have once been 'heave-y' in the lines 'Now the heavy ploughman snores/All with weary task foredone').[102] Thus, in Hopkins' case, the slack syllables are not a 'gabble' without 'structural duty'; they are part of a system which allows for the kind of interplay possible between the speaking voice and the fixed units of poetry.

Hopkins feared he would be misread; instead of trusting to the reader's ear he often marked stresses, and sometimes, as we have seen, did more; he caused confusion, and still does. The first immediate consequence was that a Jesuit whom the editor of *The Month* consulted about 'The Wreck of the Deutschland' went away with a headache, at a loss to know if he was reading the poem in the way Hopkins intended.[103] The problem persists, and is, I think, an insoluble one. Together with some of the points raised above in my discussion of sprung rhythm, it has been treated at length and to Hopkins' cost by Elizabeth Schneider in her forceful book *The Dragon in the Gate*, where she says that Hopkins seems to have handled the relation between sound and sense in a way that was arbitrary. She gives examples of Hopkins' marking of stresses on weak words and points to the oddness of this in support of her view. Amongst others she lists 'I wálk, I líft up, Í lift úp heart, eýes' (MS B, 'Hurrahing in Harvest'),[104] 'self ín self steepèd and páshed – quíte' and 'thóughts agaínst thoughts ín groans grínd' ('Spelt from Sibyl's Leaves'), and – most singular of all – 'Their ránsom, théir rescue, ánd first, fást, last friénd' ('The Lantern out of Doors').[105] If one thinks of a stress simply as a matter of relative emphasis, the effect of reading the lines in the way marked would be grotesque – if it could be done at all. One's natural assumption would be that Hopkins also would have found them grotesque – or impossible – so read; however, Professor Schneider takes the pessimistic view and supports her case by pointing to the way Hopkins handled Bridges' 'London Snow'. He wrote:

I have a few suggestions to make about the rhythm of *London Snow*, which would make it perfect...I suppose you scan 'The éye márvelled – márvelled at the dázzling whíteness; the éar héarkened to the stíllness of the sólemn áir': this is well enough when seen, but the following is easier to catch and somewhat better in itself – 'Eye márvelled – márvelled át the dázzling whiteness; ear heárkened to the stillness ín the sólemn áir'.[106]

(Hopkins has other suggestions but we may focus on this one as representative.) It is interesting to set this beside another example of his going against orthodoxy. Writing to Canon Dixon about the ways in which the English sonnet might be given more weight, he says of a piece by Gray,

(This sonnet is remarkable for its falling or trochaic rhythm –
    In | vain to | me the | smiling | mornings | shine –
and not
    In vain | to me | the smil | ing morn | ings shine)[107]

In the examples from both Gray and Bridges Hopkins shows full well that he knows how the lines can – and probably will – be managed and then he does something different. In fact the lines from Bridges give less difficulty than those from Hopkins' own work.

If we abandon accents and use great colons at critical points we get:

> Eye marvelled – marvelled **:** at the dazzling whiteness;
> Ear hearkened to the stillness **:** in the solemn air.

The stress on 'at' and 'in' is made possible by pausing before them, and the pausing contributes to the marvelling and the stillness by stopping speech at the crucial moments. As we have seen before, Hopkins' marks involve time.

To review the question: some of Hopkins' stress-marks seem inexplicable inasmuch as they are impossible to manage *as stresses only* without eradicating the meaning of a line; moreover, they involve emphasising unimportant words, and their presence seems to point to a disquieting disregard for good sense. Are we then to suppose that his ear and ours are so markedly different that all his metrical achievements are happy accidents (for it is certainly the case that a twentieth-century reader can speak his poems without difficulty if the sometimes puzzling marks are ignored)? Hardly, for Hopkins' departures from orthodoxy are certainly not the incompetence of the tyro but the choice of a master (to my knowledge, no one contests his metrical abilities). The question must remain an open one, but it can be suggested by way of tentative explanation that the effect of the stresses he marked would be to act as a brake on the pace at which the poem was taken. It seems almost certain from his few instructions on how individual poems should be read that he would have spoken them much more slowly and heavily than we would be inclined to. This notion of the puzzling stress-marks acting as a brake is in accord with that and also with Hopkins' whole effort to make the sonnet heavier (sprung rhythm allows the line to be lengthened much beyond its pentameter norm and thus makes the sonnet the bigger unit Hopkins wanted it to be); however, the conclusive evidence of Hopkins' recorded voice is not available so these remarks are conjectural. Once more, though, we should be cautious about supposing our insights to be preferable to the poet's. To look at a piece of sculpture from only one side and obstinately demand 'Why is it not like other paintings?' would be to refuse enlightenment: Hopkins' interest in the spoken and in music is part of a quest for a poetry which is richer in significance than it otherwise would be, not poorer.

Sprung rhythm was a means by which Hopkins could 'make verse stressy', and, by discarding those slack syllables which a more conventional metre would have obliged him to employ, to make the most of what he felt to be the essential power and character of the language, its 'muscle'. But a verse which deals only with power thus conceived may strike the reader as violent or as wearisomely importunate (doubtless Yeats was thinking of this when he referred to Hopkins' 'slight constant excitement'),[108] and these are the risks which Hopkins takes more than any others. However, another element in the character of the language as Hopkins conceived it is its capacity to produce a balance of similarity and difference in sound ('All beauty', he said, 'may by a metaphor be called rhyme').[109] The selectiveness of sprung rhythm is complemented in Hopkins by the exacting disciplines of Welsh poetry; as sprung rhythm allows for freer disposition of syllables within the line, so Welsh poetry has in it devices which depend upon such manoeuvrability inasmuch as their relative positioning is fixed.

On 28 August 1874, as part of his training for the priesthood, Hopkins moved to St Beuno's College in North Wales. The following day he wrote to his father that he had 'half a mind to get up a little Welsh'.[110] This he did,[111] but 'not with very pure [i.e. priestly] intentions perhaps',[112] so that he gave it up soon after starting. However, he resumed his study,[113] and two years later, when a silver jubilee album was being compiled for the Bishop of Shrewsbury, Hopkins wrote again that 'For the Welsh they had to come to me, for, sad to say, no one else in the house knows anything about it.'[114] Thus, although he wrote to Baillie in January 1877 that he could make little way with Welsh poetry,[115] he had already written a poem in Welsh, a cywydd, which indicates some grasp of the principles on which Welsh verse was founded. This is confirmed by his mention to Dixon that 'The Wreck of the Deutschland' had 'certain chimes suggested by the Welsh poetry I had been reading (what they call cynghanedd)',[116] and by his comment of 1882 on 'The Sea and the Skylark' that 'It was written in my Welsh days, in my salad days, when I was fascinated with cynghanedd or consonant-chime.'[117]

Though Hopkins' comment suggests that the fascination was

something later outgrown, the influence of Welsh poetry is discernible in his work right up to the time of his death. Indeed, it is interesting to look at Hopkins' work in the light of the following outline:

The style is exclamatory rather than predicative; such minor but useful parts of speech as articles, prepositions, pronouns, and the copula are freely dispensed with, and even the finite verb is used sparingly, its place being taken by the verb-noun. Constant use is made of compound words, both nouns and adjectives ...[and] such verbal devices as *cynghanedd*, rhyme, assonance, and alliteration[118]

A fair description of the technical features of Hopkins' mature verse; but, in fact, these words are from H. I. Bell's *The Development of Welsh Poetry* and apply to the Welsh bardic traditions of the twelfth to the sixteenth centuries. This sketch gives some idea of the striking similarities between the verse of the man who styled himself 'Brân Manaefa'[119] and the bardic poetry he studied, and these have been explored in detail in a valuable article by Gweneth Lilly.[120] Her conclusion is that Hopkins' reading of Welsh poetry was a stimulus to his experimentation rather than its first cause, but we are left in little doubt by what she has to say that Hopkins learnt important parts of his craft from the bards. What follows is essentially a short summary of Miss Lilly's essay.

The idea of *cynghanedd* was Hopkins' chief debt to the bards. He was particularly fond of *cynghanedd sain*, a device involving three divisions in the line, of which the first two have syllables which rhyme and the last two have syllables which alliterate. These are examples (asterisks mark alliteration, italics mark rhyme):

> our sor*did* tur*bid* time ('The Sea and the Skylark')
>
> Left *hand*, off *land*, I hear the lark (*ibid.*)
>
> I awoke in the Midsummer not-to-call *night*, | in the *white* and the *walk* of the morning ('Moonrise')

Plainly, this chiming of consonants need not be kept to this strict pattern to be effective. Miss Lilly gives

> And *wears* man's smudge and *shares* man's smell ('God's Grandeur')

as an example in Hopkins of the easier *cynghanedd sain godwynog*.
Other variations are possible. In

> *Banned* by the *land* of their birth ('The Wreck of the Deutschland', stanza 21)

he makes the first and third units alliterate instead of the second and third. Other combinations of rhyme and alliteration used by Hopkins are not traditional in Welsh. Thus,

All the *air* things *wear* that build this world of Wales ('In the Valley of the Elwy')

and

Fall, gall themselves, and gash gold-vermilion ('The Windhover')

are his own developments, and in

that *toil*, that *coil*, since (seems) I kissed ('Carrion Comfort')

the *cynghanedd* pattern is interrupted by an independent alliterative one. In

Warm-laid grave of a womb-life grey ('The Wreck of the Deutschland', stanza 7)

and

wind-wandering weed-winding ('Binsey Poplars')

the pattern of consonants used in the first phrase is used in the second.

Miss Lilly finds precedents in Welsh for Hopkins' use of the verb-noun ('soft sift', 'a lonely began'), for tmesis ('wind-lilylocks-laced', 'brim, in a flash, full'), for his interruption of a sentence by an exclamation ('hurls for him, O half hurls earth for him', 'Where we, even where we mean / To mend her'), and for his alliteration of two pairs of initial consonants (e.g. 'grave' and 'grey'). But she points out that, despite these and other similarities, Hopkins' early verse with its compounds such as 'pansy-dark', 'dainty-delicate', 'plum-purple' ('A Vision of the Mermaids') and its separation of adjective and noun, as in 'The Habit of Perfection' –

> And lily-coloured *clothes* provide
> Your spouse *not laboured-at nor spun*

– already shows Hopkins moving in the direction later encouraged by his reading of Welsh.[121] If we were to look for the chief technical influence on Hopkins, Welsh would have a stronger claim than Anglo-Saxon verse - the language of which Hopkins began to learn only seven years before his death[122] (and which verse shows 'a superficial resemblance')[123] – but still,

There is reason to believe that, even if Hopkins had never gone to St. Beuno's, had never studied Welsh poetry, his mature work would have contained instances of internal rhyme, half-rhyme, and alliteration, but they would not have been found in the same profusion, or in such a variety of patterns.[124]

In Welsh poetry Hopkins' double need to find the distinctiveness he wanted for his own work and to escape from the poetic conventions then current was partly supplied. It provided the impersonal authority of an established tradition that was nonetheless quite distinct from any post-Romantic movement in nineteenth-century English poetry. The bards gave one answer to his fervent desire for exacting discipline and individuality of style.

It was hard to hold a middle way in his age. He read Bridges' *Ulysses*, full of Greek gods, 'totally unworkable material', and jibed, 'What did Athene do after leaving Ulysses? Lounged back to Olympus to afternoon nectar.'[125] Against such literary self-involvement Hopkins was resolute; but there were other traps. Tennyson was tempted astray by the thought of a platform presence for poetry (I think of 'Locksley Hall Sixty Years After'), of a verse subservient to the felt needs of public rhetoric: Hopkins' pre-occupation with form is a sign of his conviction that poetry has to justify itself instead by what it is and not in terms of service to some external end. If, in acting on that conviction, he sometimes seems capricious or mannered, his own apology is still apposite: 'make him understand that those snags that are in my style are not in my heart and temper'.[126]

4

Eternal May-time

As sure as what is most sure,[1] sure as that spring primroses
Shall new-dapple next year[1]

Hopkins' poetry ebbed and flowed according to the various postings
which his Society gave him. It is no coincidence, then, that much of
his most confident work was written in Wales, where he was happiest.
It was for him 'the loveable west',[2] 'the true Arcadia of wild beauty',[3]
and 'always to me a mother of Muses'.[4] When he spent a holiday
there in 1886 as a brief respite from the strains of his work in Ireland
he swiftly recovered his happiness and his excitement. 'If you have
not seen Pont Aberglaslyn in sunlight', he told Bridges, 'you have
something to live for'.[5] However, behind these fluctuations according to circumstance lies the polarity in Hopkins' mind which so
attracted him to Parmenides' teaching on Being and Not-being, a
polarity (explored in this chapter and the next) which shows in his
poetry as spring and death.

Spring is for Hopkins a condition rather than a season. He does
not treat it as a passing from winter nor as a movement towards
autumn, and it is hardly distinct from summer for him, which is
why, with some licence, I group poems such as 'Hurrahing in
Harvest' under this head. Hopkins' nature poems are poems about
the growing time of year and the strong and lively youthfulness of
man. In winter, in age, he was scarcely interested. Indeed, there is
much in his own poetic creativeness which is seasonal: apart from
the one true winter poem he wrote ('The Wreck of the Deutschland'),
where the hostility and difficulty of the dark months are inseparable
from the fact of the wreck which occurred in them, the bulk of his

work seems to have come from the spring–summer of the year. 'God's Grandeur' and 'The Starlight Night' were written in February but, though there is a wintery drabness in the 'brown brink' of 'God's Grandeur' and a chill in the 'grey lawns cold' of the other, in each case we are soon back to spring in the Holy Ghost's brooding hen-warmth over the world and the May orchards to which he compares the stars.

There is something both idealistic and wistful in Hopkins' preoccupation; idealistic because it is easier to propose the visible operation of a loving God in the world when there is plain and natural evidence of warmth and beauty and vitality, and wistful because Hopkins wanted it so all the time. There is a major limitation on him here (the limitation some point to by calling him a 'nature poet',[6] others by saying he was 'innocent'),[7] a limitation in range of mood and feeling which excludes the intuitive difficulties involved in confronting a nature which has the tiger as well as the lamb, which is sometimes 'red in tooth and claw' – the nature, more recently, of the stabbing 'attent sleek thrushes' (unlike the birds of Ted Hughes, the thrush in Hopkins' poetry sings – no more). The limitation is of apparent not-knowingness; but it was freely chosen and not the actual boundary of his poetic talent. He could handle superbly the complications of adversity (as we shall see he did in Ireland), and there is nothing more powerful or moving than the nature poetry of the thirteenth stanza of 'The Wreck of the Deutschland', which quite obviously does not describe the contained and comfortable nature of pretty things. Why did he work, then, within such narrow confines? For answer we must return to the wistfulness in him.

It is the wistfulness of a solitary and, as such, need not endure the constraint of public opinion; it is the wistfulness, in part, of someone in retreat who has recourse to nature as a sanctuary from what is in humanity unmanageable or disagreeable. The Hopkins whose monasticism in explicitly religious matters was sacrificed to the instructions of the Society of Jesus finds satisfaction in natural experiences which, as he treats them, become religious. He is in this in the pejorative sense romantic, discovering in the scene before him the serenity which escapes him in his dealings with people; but that lack of serenity is so little stated in the mature poetry that the full significance of the choice is obscured. (We are not dealing in Hopkins with that other romanticism which finds rural life more real than urban, or which discovers in the pastoral communal life of the Lake District, as De Quincey did, a 'monastic peace'.) Nature is an alternative to society. This much is plain in the early 'The Alchemist in the City'. Joined with the Alchemist's fruitless experimentation (which is offered, unconvincingly, as its cause) is

> The incapable and cumbrous shame
> Which makes me when with men I deal
> More powerless than the blind or lame.

The two, the professional failure and the gaucheness, are sufficient to send the Alchemist's thoughts out of the city to the wilderness, and

> There on a long and squarèd height
> After the sunset I would lie,
> And pierce the yellow waxen light
> With free long looking, ere I die.

The romantic comes to this gesture out of a felt inferiority; the poem is plain about that.

However, in the mature work this is transmuted. Hopkins has become a spectator in a direct antagonism between nature in its scenic manifestations and man; and his sympathies are with nature. Thus, in a poem which, with its moon and its roar of the sea, is Hopkins' 'Dover Beach' (except that, where Arnold is bewildered, Hopkins knows exactly what is amiss), he says of the sea and the skylark,

> How these two shame this shallow and frail town!
>   How ring right out our sordid turbid time,
> Being pure!

The shallowness and frailty, the sordidness and turbidity, we have to take on trust, but certainly Hopkins does not exclude himself from the complaint – he is not being careless with accusations. He is primarily implicated in a different way, though. He is in the difficulty of all whose insights seem to them preferable to other people's; merely by recognising the communal squalor and shallowness he tends to dissociate himself from it – he has seen something better and is something better for having seen it (a feature Hopkins identified in himself, and checked, in 'The Candle Indoors').

The experience of nature is an alternative to the experience of society, and it is a better alternative. In 'The Sea and the Skylark' this is true because nature is more 'pure'; in 'Hurrahing in Harvest' nature is more real. This is that poem's second quatrain:

> I walk, I lift up, I lift up heart, eyes,
> Down all that glory in the heavens to glean our Saviour;
> And, éyes, heárt, what looks, what lips yet gave you a
> Rapturous love's greeting of realer, of rounder replies?

What welcome was ever more friendly, more frank, more 'real' than this 'greeting' of Christ in the cloud shapes and the wheat stooks? What human contact could ever be as trustworthy as this? As in the details of a face closely beheld, nature is companionable. One would hardly expect Hopkins to be eager, then, to write about the sort of nature which is challenging or repugnant. Having located one reason for Hopkins' selectiveness, it is necessary to postpone for a little any discussion of what should follow – his sacramentalism – with the brief acknowledgement here that, if spring is companionable (and it is eternal also), the kind of scene which follows now is sorely at odds with it:

Under a stone hedge was a dying ram: there ran slowly from his nostril a thick flesh-coloured ooze, scarlet in places, coiling and roping its way down, so thick that it looked like fat[8]

We should acquit Hopkins of gentility, which is one of the risks such selectiveness entails.

He was a solitary in his experience of nature (there is not even, as there is in Arnold, a reaper or herdsman to challenge the solitude), and where the solitariness breeds whimsical notions it harms the poetry. A solitary may be a visionary – or he may be a dreamer:

> Look at the stars! look, look up at the skies!
> O look at all the fire-folk sitting in the air!
> The bright boroughs, the circle-citadels there!
> Down in dim woods the diamond delves! the elves'-eyes!
> The grey lawns cold where gold, where quickgold lies!

One looks in vain in 'The Starlight Night' for any sort of mature discretionary check on the fancifulness which is the chief mode through which the stars are experienced. There is considerable skill deployed in accurately observing the night sky – in places it is made grey by the profusion of dimmer stars against which one or two ('gold') stand out more brightly, and these places are likened to lawns on a clear frosty night (the 'Down' which is the solitary and inadequate reason some have found for moving our attention earthward at this point did not occur in the version Hopkins sent to his mother)[9] – but this is overwhelmed by talk of fairies and diamond mining (a traditionally elfin labour) deep in woods. Childhood wonder is refreshing in a grown man but not sufficient in a poet (in whom we look for a development of feeling), and, without some answering acknowledgement on his part that it is just that, it may strike us as not so much fresh as naive, unknowing. The whole man is not involved here. As Hopkins was to say of those who write a deliberately archaic language, 'he is at something else than the seeming matter in hand'.[10] So he is himself – in the sestet – claiming for the religion of the martyr the provinces of fairyland:

> These are indeed the barn; withindoors house
> The shocks. This piece-bright paling shuts the spouse
> Christ home, Christ and his mother and all his hallows.

Nature in this poem is untouchable, protected by more than vast distance, for it is conceived of either in terms of elfin magic, quite unapproachable for humans, or as the actualisation of the Biblical trope of Christ's barn, protectively garnering all believers. With a metaphor, with a theology, no vandal can cope.

In 'The Starlight Night', then, Hopkins' wistfulness results in a whimsicality which is then jerked into a token service of his faith, auctioneered ('Buy then! bid then!') into a false exchange of prayers for beauty, when the beauty is anyway free and the prayers are more like religious trappings than a heartfelt asking. Yet he had already written in a letter to his mother, 'no one is ever so poor that he is not (without prejudice to all the rest of the world) owner of the skies and stars and everything wild that is to be found on the earth':[11] in his poem Hopkins seeks to qualify this ownership and impose a meaning on it.

The wistfulness in Hopkins had a profounder base than this; his monasticism is not simply a retreat, it is a judgement on centuries of numbing commercialism which are the sign of the fundamental discord between man and the world he lives in:

> The world is charged with the grandeur of God.
>   It will flame out, like shining from shook foil;
>   It gathers to a greatness, like the ooze of oil
> Crushed. Why do men then now not reck his rod?
> Generations have trod, have trod, have trod;
>   And all is seared with trade; bleared, smeared with toil;
>   And wears man's smudge and shares man's smell: the soil
> Is bare now, nor can foot feel, being shod.

The judgement is not simply on '*our* sordid turbid time' (my italics); it is a judgement on history, the history of a filthy and destructive civilisation, 'founded', Hopkins had said in a letter, 'on wrecking',[12] and oblivious to the access of the power of beauty present in the natural world. 'Generations' (a long, ruminative word, evocative of the weight of ages' habitual grossness) 'have trod, have trod, have trod' in the heavy marked footfalls which are at once the deadening, regular pounding of tramping feet and the repetition of such pounding through the years, a repetition re-enforced in the internal rhyme of 'seared...bleared, smeared' and the alliteration of 'smudge' and 'smell'.

Written in an age of 'half-believers', 'God's Grandeur' is startling and impressive in its confidence. It is unequivocal, presenting religious belief as empirical fact in the three unqualified assertions with which the octave opens, and possessed of the cumulative force which comes from the sensuously detailed way they are presented. The particular skill of the opening lines lies in the way the fact of being charged is so fully demonstrated. God's grandeur is metaphorically akin to electric current, which also has the quality of existing in a way that is invisible yet there for the senses, a source of enormous power. This idea is further extended in the second line with the simile of light reflected off shaken metal foil, and the other sense of 'charged', brim-full, is developed in the gathering ooze of oil. However, the two similes are sufficiently different to indicate that the grandeur they describe is more than a question of visible glory: there is an implication in it which the sequence of logic, the sequence picked out by 'then', makes the justifying factor in man's obedience – why has he not taken notice? Remarkably, a brutalised sensibility which shows in an inability to sense the physical world and in the blunt, preoccupied busyness of commerce and labour is made the sign of man's apostasy. This is not Christian teaching – one has to remind oneself – it is Hopkins'; and perhaps an even wider departure is present in the ambiguous syntax of the poem, for, if the statement about generations is there not just to re-enforce the question 'Why do men...not reck his rod?' but as an answer to it, Hopkins is making the brutalisation not just a sign of disobedience but, in a practical way, its cause. Like Ruskin, Hopkins could not but feel that beauty and morality were connected: on any reading of the poem, disobedience to God is here a matter of aesthetic sensibility. Moreover, there is, in this poem, no feeling that the situation is remediable. The focus of the sestet is firmly set on the power of nature's survival; it is inexhaustible, victorious; which leaves man defeated but unchanged, still unconnected. 'Bent/World' is a visual description of the horizon, but it applies also to the world's moral condition, distorted out of true, and likely to remain so because of the very rigidity which 'bent' connotes. From the bare soil of the octave through 'the dearest freshness deep down things' of the sestet to the springing of the eastward sun one has the sense of the deeply buried, deeply protected, newly awakening seed, but man has passed out of view; the poet contemplates alone.

When Hopkins' attention was focussed on some small particular in the natural world he felt acutely its vulnerability, and this is so in 'Binsey Poplars', where the insensitivity chastised in 'God's Grandeur' has become something more like purposeful malice. The felling of trees is likened to horrible mutilation:

> That, like this sleek and seeing ball
> But a prick will make no eye at all

Like the hewn timber, the blinded eye still exists as an object, but its essential nature (its ability, we may say, to put the world inside the head) is destroyed. However, in the larger view, the 'dearest freshness' is eternal. Endlessly regenerative, beyond the reach of time, it was a great solace to Hopkins whenever intuitively he could feel in contact with it (although many times this was not so for him, harassed and hurt by 'Thousands of thorns, thoughts'). The perpetual life of nature, caught in 'God's Grandeur' in the diurnal revolution of the earth, is a reminder of what might have been. The yearnings of a city-dweller in industrial England for things to be as they were before the advent of spoil-tips and pollution become in Hopkins a wish for something out of time altogether.

'Spring' is

A strain of the earth's sweet being in the beginning
In Eden garden

and it is that conviction which puts Hopkins' poetry into a transcendental time scale. He is not concerned with our littlenesses; for all his particular observations, his view is grand and extensive. Thus, in 'Spring', time gone is not time before the smoke-stacks and factories but time of the age of innocence. Hopkins' persistent theme is a calling back of mankind, never a vision of some future wholly different from past or present. There is a simple kind of conservatism in this as well as a moral concern. The backward glances which Tennyson and Arnold and Browning gave to other societies (real and supposed), and which Morris turned into a persistent gaze, have a small place in his poetry as well. Thus, in 'Duns Scotus's Oxford' the affection which Hopkins feels for the schoolman is subsumed in the larger attraction which Scotus' period has: the 'base and brickish' inessentials are lost from sight as nineteenth-century Oxford becomes, not a survival, but 'these weeds and waters, these walls' of the medieval city, 'haunted' by the scholar still. 'Harry Ploughman' with its feeling of 'churlsgrace' might be a description of a feudal labourer. However, the general effect of these details is to remind us that Hopkins' feeling of 'the hollowness of this century's civilisation'[13] shows in his poetry as it shows in that of his contemporaries – in absence.

When one considers Hopkins' view of man, the difficulties posed by his Catholicism become critical: there are careful discriminations to be made.

Plainly, much more is involved in Christianity than the giving of assent to certain received teachings. The doctrines, once held, become dynamic in the life of a believer; this is no simple process, and it is with the character of the process that the disinterested critic of a Christian poet is concerned. For example, a man does not spontaneously love his neighbour simply because the instruction to do so is divinely endorsed: he may not *will* himself to feel. He may change his actions, for these he largely controls, but there will always be a gap between conviction and feeling. Indeed, unless one admits to the existence of such a gap, I do not know how, on a mundane level, one is to describe the presence of sin in the life of a believer. It is not within man's unaided power to close the gap: only God-given grace can do that. Christianity is never a fully accomplished fact in an individual's earthly life (sin would be excluded from that life if it were); it is an aspiration, a lodestone pull.

If it is worth anything, a Christian poet's work is, then, never a simple reiteration of doctrine, for doctrines are public and general; it is about his experience of the doctrine realised dynamically in his life, and, because that realisation will be incomplete and a matter of change and development, it is possible for a non-believer intuitively to comprehend the impulses involved in the aspiration without sharing the goal. Moreover, a development in faith is inextricable from a development in feeling.

This seems to me to be well shown within the corpus of one poem in George Herbert's fine 'Redemption':

> Having been tenant long to a rich Lord,
>   Not thriving, I resolved to be bold,
>   And make a suit unto him, to afford
> A new small-rented lease, and cancell th'old.
> In heaven at his manour I him sought:
>   They told me there, that he was lately gone
>   About some land, which he had dearly bought
> Long since on earth, to take possession.
> I straight return'd, and knowing his great birth,
>   Sought him accordingly in great resorts;
>   In cities, theatres, gardens, parks, and courts:
> At length I heard a ragged noise and mirth
>   Of theeves and murderers: there I him espied,
>   Who straight, *Your suit is granted*, said, & died.

Beginning with all the expectations of a narrow Old Testament legalism, the dissatisfied tenant in the poem looks for his lord – high, mighty, and forbidding – with whom he hopes to arrange a new contract. The lord is not at home. He is out on business, his absence seemingly betokening the bland indifference with which the high treat the low. That such elusiveness is something quite other than self-involved unawareness of the supplicant's wants is soon to be demonstrated, however, though the supplicant has yet to realise this. He pursues his search, quite misconstruing the real nature of the highness and mightiness of the lord for whom he is looking, and his search is a failure – he has looked in all the wrong places. When the two do meet, the encounter is seemingly accidental and quite unconnected with the supplicant's futile initiatives. This is not at all the formal audience he had envisaged. His lord is indeed approachable now, but how could he now persist with his own self-centred suit to one in such a dire predicament, scoffed at and surrounded by murderers? There is no need. Unprompted, speaking even here amongst the mob with the poise and command of a ruler, and in words the mere knowingness of which shows that all the while the supplicant's little purpose was subsumed in a far greater one, the lord grants the unspoken plea; and it costs him his life. The aspirant's business view of existence, advanced in the flat, passionless tones of the poem, will never be adequate again: he has experienced what the upright laws of commerce never could contain, a love of him that passes understanding.

More could be said, for the lord is, of course, the crucified Redeemer whose blood was spilt in the making of a new covenant, but my point about doctrine becoming dynamic and its dynamism being the thing of consequence for poetry may perhaps be clearer now. It is a matter of the general, the doctrine, being interiorised and made particular and alive as it is mediated through the feelings and intelligence of the individual poet (the impact of Herbert's poem on the reader depends thus on a sort of rediscovery from the inside of something he knew before). When Hopkins writes about man I do not find such an interiorisation of doctrine, and this seems to me his severest limitation as a poet. Christianity involves the acceptance of the contrary-working judgements that man is both a child of God and a sinner, not one or the other but both simultaneously (it is not surprising that other moral systems have taken an apparently easier way out by separating off innocence and fixing guilt outside man in his environment). In my view, this difficult simultaneity eluded Hopkins because his own acutely developed aesthetic sense supervened. Whatever alignments may be made by individual Christians, Christian doctrine offers no teaching on aesthetics, but Hopkins personally could not disregard the beauty of things. As we have seen, he conceived of that beauty as witnessing to the creative purpose and presence of God, and he tied beauty of body in man to primal innocence. There are, consequentially, difficulties in loving the unlovely, or in acknowledging that handsome people are sinners still (acknowledging, that is, as something more than head-truth, what this means). Moreover, in the insight it contains, the ambivalence in the Christian view of man is not unique. Though people outside the Christian belief would not speak of 'sin', and 'innocence' might be a smaller word for them than it would be for Christians, they might yet hold the feeling that a potential in man to be better than he has been co-exists in him with a capability for sinking lower still. Between the romanticism of holding the one and the cynicism of holding the other as the sole and all-inclusive truth lies wisdom. In Hopkins we have oscillation, and that seems to me to be a characteristic of him, and not of the faith to which he subscribed.

This oscillation is ultimately for him one between beauty and ugliness. On the ugliness we have this:

> While I admired the handsome horses I remarked for the thousandth time with sorrow and loathing the base and bespotted figures and features of the Liverpool crowd. When I see the fine and manly Norwegians that flock hither to embark for America walk our streets and look about them it fills me with shame and wretchedness[14]

and this:

> What I most dislike in towns and in London in particular is the misery of the poor; the dirt, squalor, and the illshapen degraded physical (putting aside moral) type of so many of the people, with the deeply dejecting, unbearable thought that by degrees almost all our population will become a town population and a puny unhealthy and cowardly one.[15]

These comments are seven years apart, but both issue into the same complaint about supposed British cowardice before the Boers at the Battle of Majuba. That, their consistency, and mention in the first quotation of 'the thousandth time', show that they are representative of Hopkins' general attitude and are not impulsive judgements. As such, what is dismaying about them is that they are so external. 'Misery' is synonymous most immediately not with suffering but with 'dirt, squalor, and the illshapen degraded physical. . .type'. Are the poor victims, or culprits? Hopkins never even arrives at that question because poverty itself so offends as a spectacle that it paralyses analysis (the facile transference from ugliness to cowardice is hardly analysis). The easy reductive juxtaposition of horses and people and the simple opposition of 'base and bespotted' with 'fine and manly' are signs of the superficiality that in turn betokens want of imaginative hold on the inner lives of the people he surveys. 'Loathing' of 'figures and features' are not the terms in which consciousness of sin presents itself: the revulsion is personal to Hopkins, and it is a revulsion at ugliness. On the beauty Hopkins writes:

> Í say more: the just man justices;
>   Keeps gráce: thát keeps all his goings graces;
> Acts in God's eye what in God's eye he is –
>   Chríst. For Christ plays in ten thousand places,
> Lovely in limbs, and lovely in eyes not his
>   To the Father through the features of men's faces.

This, the sestet to 'As kingfishers catch fire', gives the doctrine of divine grace in a singleness of being and doing; but men are not dragonflies to flash thus simply in the sun, and the limbs through which Christ plays may be withered or mutilated, the features ugly. With the complication that man, even as he has the Christ-potential within him, may yet put the nails in the cross, the attractive emotions of this poem are not adequate to cope.

Hopkins' insistence on man's depredations is part of his general reluctance to conceive of him in any terms other than those indicated by his ideal role. 'Earth's eye, tongue, or heart' is 'dear and dogged man' ('Ribblesdale'); he is nature's 'clearest-selvèd spark' ('That Nature is a Heraclitean Fire'), 'world's loveliest' ('To what serves Mortal Beauty?') and 'life's pride and cared-for crown' ('The Sea and the Skylark'). He is, in Hopkins' eyes, like the windhover, one of God's beautiful creatures; but he has failed in that role, and Hopkins' feelings become tangled in the contradiction between what he is and what he should be, so that Hopkins prefers to state the contradiction rather than to deal with a truth considerably more complex than this. In 'The Sea and the Skylark' he says,

> We, life's pride and cared-for crown,
> Have lost that cheer and charm of earth's past prime:
> Our make and making break, are breaking, down
> To man's last dust, drain fast towards man's first slime.

'Men, he thought, had sprung from slime', Hopkins noted of Parmenides,[16] but what is of consequence here is not this idea but the extremeness of the choice between 'slime' and 'crown'. Hopkins has but simple propositions to advance; the communal, the traditional, the shared historical processes of a culture are outside his attention, for, on this subject, his is a poetry without inflection. His view firm set on the next world, he announces the fragility and vacuity of congregated man, man so intent on himself as (in 'Ribblesdale')

> To thriftless reave both our rich round world bare
> And none reck of world after,

man defined by his failure to 'correspond' ('In the Valley of the Elwy'), in servitude to passing time, 'day-labouring out life's age' ('The Caged Skylark').

He found it easier to write about Man than men, and this for reasons which are inextricably a mixture of biography and belief. In his poetry he carries his idealism into his feelings for individuals. When, in 'The Loss of the Eurydice', he speaks of the ship's crew as 'the breathing temple' (line 93) one feels his limitations: anyone who has that view of man will find it hard to avoid either sentimentality or bitter disappointment. Indeed, it is Hopkins' wish to discover man in his ideal aspect that takes him to youth and beauty and the strength and innocence of youth. Hopkins' poems about people are poems about spring in their life:

> Have, get, before it cloy,
> Before it cloud, Christ, lord, and sour with sinning,
> Innocent mind and Mayday in girl and boy,
> Most, O maid's child, thy choice and worthy the winning.
>
>   ('Spring')

'Most. . .*thy* choice'? Most Hopkins' choice; and an understandable but, to him as a poet, a very limiting one. Youth's energy and idealism and openness to experience are very attractive; its moodiness, callowness and impetuosity are unmentioned in Hopkins, as is the appealing, mature wisdom of age.

There is, however, more to the limitation than this. His poems about people are for the most part poems about boys and men. 'The Handsome Heart', 'The Bugler's First Communion', 'Felix Randal', 'Brothers', 'The Soldier', 'Harry Ploughman', 'To what serves Mortal Beauty?' – there are enough of them on similar subjects to indicate a narrowing of the range of interest still further. They point to the homosexual feelings in him whose presence is, in my view, conclusively established by his unpublished confession-notes.[17] Inevitably tensions must have been set up in him by feelings not publicly avowable or privately assuring to him, and I think it reasonable to suggest that these aggravated that sense of his distinctiveness which he had and which contributed to his feeling of loneliness in Ireland. How deep the tensions ran and how persistent they were is a matter for the biographer, however. It seems to me that only in one place can it be maintained with confidence that they run in the poetry, and here again one encounters Hopkins' sacramentalism, that collapse of perspectives which comes from seeing everything as actually or potentially holy.

The poem is 'To what serves Mortal Beauty?'. (It is a question which Pater or Swinburne would have found strange, and which Hopkins' own poetry would not normally accommodate *as* a question.) In it Hopkins uses his sacramentalism to answer the special and personal problem. The poem deals with emotions (for women – or for men, and here they are for men) that one would expect a celibate priest to have sometimes to contend with (Hopkins himself tells the story of the bishop who, when told by clergy that they had intellectual difficulties in the way of remaining in the priesthood, would reply 'What is her name?').[18] Indeed, the problem is such that it receives no fuller development than a bald statement; the blood may dance outside the poem at the beauty of a body, but it does not do so within it. Severely, the question is truncated to admit the confident-seeming answer. It is a reply which gives the private feeling public dignity, of a man drawn to boys by their beauty, the precedent of the Forum 'Non Angli sed angeli'. This is gracious, with its 'lovely lads' who are, in the language of spring–summer, 'wet-fresh windfalls of war's storm'; but it is irrelevant to the problem of passion, as we see in the sestet:

> Our law says: Love what are¹ love's worthiest, were all known;
> World's loveliest – men's selves. Self¹ flashes off frame and face.

Love frame and face, then; that is not what the poem says, for Hopkins stops before this, the crucial step, but it is where the logic impels. Instead, Hopkins resists the inertia which takes one to that meaning and goes into the emptiness of 'merely meet it' and the intellectual and emotional shut-down of 'let that alone'.

The 'angels' on whom Gregory's gaze fell could, in Hopkins' treatment of them, have included the bugler at his first communion, the dead sailor 'all of a lovely manly mould' in 'The Loss of the Eurydice', Harry Ploughman or – in his health – Felix Randal, for outside their immediate situations they are interchangeable, without personality; they are types. Their type is of young manliness; it is of Christ the hero, to whom Hopkins gave attributes which only the more emphasise his own limits. Christ was in his body 'most beautiful', a stranger to sickness, 'the greatest genius that ever lived', tender yet stern as he chose, and thus to be feared. The leader thus described to the people of Bedford Leigh¹⁹ – a superman rather than a shepherd – is the one we meet in 'The Soldier', where Hopkins is trying himself to come to terms with the consequences of his sacramentalism.

> Yes. Whý do we áll, seeing of a soldier, bless him? bless
> Our redcoats, our tars? Both these being, the greater part,
> But frail clay, nay but foul clay. Here it is: the heart,
> Since, proud, it calls the calling manly, gives a guess
> That, hopes that, makesbelieve, the men must be no less;
> It fancies, feigns, deems, dears the artist after his art;
> And fain will find as sterling all as all is smart,
> And the scarlet wear the spirit of wár thére express.

A child might have the feeling, inadequate and expressed in picture-book language ('Our redcoats, our tars'), which the poem sets out to consider, but a child would not give to it the weight of reasoning support that Hopkins does. Even in the nineteenth century we did not all 'bless' soldiers; but I think it would be wrong to suggest, by recalling, for example, Peterloo (where plainly there would have been no blessing for the Hussars and the Manchester Yeomanry), that the limitation on the poem is primarily one of class and background. The naivety which makes this such a slight piece is Hopkins' own; it shows in the initial blessing and also in his not relinquishing the very admiration with which, as the question shows, he himself is uneasy. 'Foul clay' confirms the inadequacy of 'Our redcoats, our tars' – as does the exchange of 'crown' for 'slime' – by showing an extreme instability of judgement, but 'foul clay' is not allowed to transmute the original feeling into a more educated emotion. It is of the essence of the naivety in the man that the two exist severally, never in full encounter. Though Hopkins' reasoning seems plausible enough (that, as one shapes one's impression of an artist by what one knows of his work, so one judges a soldier by the manliness of his calling), he is driven to shy away from the truth in euphemism: the only 'spirit' of war that is 'express' in 'scarlet wear' is no spirit at all; it is physical bloodshed. Hopkins was 'a very great patriot'[20] and this adulation of war is entirely consistent with that patriotism. What follows does not touch *our* sense of the real:

> Mark Christ our King. He knows war, served this soldiering through;
> He of all can reeve a rope best.

This is the prince of peace; but when Hopkins has to describe what he is talking about, he avoids the contradiction: Christ does not praise the fighting soldier, involved in bloodshed – he praises when he sees 'somewhére some mán do all that man can do'.

Hopkins has tried to explain his admiration for soldiers, but has found that it depends on a 'guess', that he only 'hopes' or 'makes-believe'. He then transfers his admiration to Christ-as-soldier, still attempting to justify the original blessing and insisting at the same time on the manliness of his own religious faith; Christ 'of all can reeve a rope best' (which is feeble evidence of manliness). The spiritual conflict which Christ fought is blurred into physical battle (by the same logic, the metaphors of the Church Militant and the Jesuit as soldier of Christ do not support Hopkins' literal statement).

In 'The Bugler's First Communion' the sentimentality he had for 'regimental red' is but one of the damaging elements in a poem which has far more failures than successes in it. It is at the confluence of strong feelings in Hopkins – for young maleness, for patriotism, for

religion – and none of them is adequately treated: the meeting was
too much for him. The emphasis of 'This very very day' marks a
thrill entirely private to Hopkins, as does the particular insistence of
'Here he knelt then ín regimental red'. The religion of 'To his
youngster take his treat' is wanting in gravity, and Christ is grotes-
quely 'fetched' from a cupboard in the elements of Communion.
The juggling of 'divine heavens' becoming in the poem 'divine,/By
it, heavens', or, later, of 'whose least quickenings lift me' becoming
'least me quickenings lift' is unjustifiable. The way in which
Hopkins picks up and drops lines of military imagery is casual. The
ranks–sally–march–comrade–dress–order language of the fifth
stanza is in service to a scene of warfare in the heavens reminiscent
of *Paradise Lost :*

> Frowning and forefending angel-warder
> Squander the hell-rook ranks sally to molest him;
>   March, kind comrade, abreast him;
> Dress his days to a dextrous and starlight order.

But this is forgotten for the mundane quartermastery of serving 'to/
Just such slips of soldiery Christ's royal ration', and that abandoned
in turn for the Arthurian romance of Hopkins' wish to see the boy
soldier 'An our day's God's own Galahad'.

The boy soldier is just like the 'breathing temple' of 'The Loss of
Eurydice' in that Hopkins wishes to see in him 'bloom of a chastity
in mansex fine'; he is also like the 'wet-fresh' boys of Gregory's
Forum since he represents 'fresh youth fretted in a bloomfall'; and
such sanctity, such wet-freshness, marks the limits of the priest's
interest in his life. Hopkins shows no sign of wanting to know of any
other dimension to his existence. The involvement presented in the
poem is, humanly, superficial; and, though it is understandable, the
spiritual faint-heartedness of

> Let mé though see no more of him, and not disappointment
> Those sweet hopes quell

is essentially self-regarding. There is no promise of compassion here
for the wayward and erring; that is Christ's business: Hopkins
would rather not know.

It is not merely fortuitous, then, that Hopkins should be seen as thinking of his religion in magical terms at one point, for magic makes human difficulties irrelevant:

> O now work well that sealing sacred ointment!
> O for now charms, arms, what bans off bad
> And locks love ever in a lad!

Magic is outside the meeting of people with people. Magic is control, and it is a resort against the usual course of nature where there is cyclic change: it evidences here Hopkins' wish to stop time at spring-time (when love is 'locked' it is 'in a lad' – there is no suggestion of aging). Equally, it is not fortuitous that at the first sign of complicating adversity in the poem (the hell-ranks represent adversity, but of a simple and self-assuring kind) Hopkins should rise to the dignity and greatness of

> I have put my lips on pleas
> Would brandle adamantine heaven with ride and jar, did
> Prayer go disregarded:

What is right *is* so, no matter what the personal consequences, the absoluteness of that right being established here by the existence of pleas independent of the lips so humbly there to reverence them – pleas awesome enough to shake heaven with their justice (the shaking, like the pleading, being a matter of substantial movement, as if of the natural properties of the material world). This is the strength we see again in Ireland in 'Thou art indeed just, Lord'.

The disappointment which 'the breathing temple' and the bugler boy warn of implicitly because they are so idealised became a fact in Hopkins' later poetry. As the dynamic unanswerable force of 'God's Grandeur' declined into the ineffectual maternalism of 'Ribblesdale' (which, like the earlier poem, also has men leaving the world 'bare' and not 'recking'), Hopkins' picture of man began to separate itself from his picture of nature. In 'That Nature is a Heraclitean Fire' the separation is evinced in the fact of direct contrast, but in 'Tom's Garland' and 'The shepherd's brow' (to be discussed in a different context) it shows in the way that ignobleness is measured against other standards than the wrecking of the natural world. Apart from noting occasional felicities, such as the easy, light-hearted swing of 'seldom sick,/Seldomer heartsore' or the physical, bramble

obstructiveness of 'thick/Thousands of thorns, thoughts', it is
difficult to make any positive claims for 'Tom's Garland', but the
very fact of Hopkins' attempt to see man socially seems to me to
mark in his case an advance. However, the kind of social vision
which is offered is of the extreme kind which always threatens as a
possibility in the other poems about people:

> This, by Despair, bred Hangdog dull; by Rage,
> Manwolf, worse; and their packs infest the age.

This is journalistic in its sensationalist generalisations. Is Hopkins'
'their packs infest the age' an attack on the unemployed or upon
their condition? Is there not, still, something very uncertain in a
poem 'upon the Unemployed' which concentrates for the most part
on a healthy labourer with a job?

> For how to the heart's cheering
> The down-dugged ground-hugged grey
> Hovers off, the jay-blue heavens appearing
> Of pied and peeled May!

So Hopkins wrote, opening the twenty-sixth stanza of 'The Wreck
of the Deutschland', and, as I indicated at the start of this chapter,
his own heart was cheered creatively by the onset of spring – it was
his chief poetic recourse. It was also a sort of intuitive therapy for
him. The life of spring is unbidden and inevitable. In Hopkins' eyes
it is easy and gentle too, and its inevitability and its gentleness were
much needed by him in Ireland when failure had become a permanent expectation for him, and when unrewarded effort and racking
introspection were chief among the features of his life.

'Patience, hard thing!' and 'My own heart let me more have pity
on' were, effectively, rejoinders to other poems he wrote on the same
sheet ('To seem the stranger' and 'I wake and feel'), and in each of
the former it is the spontaneous natural life which restores Hopkins.
He is struggling to escape from the intellect-time, death-time, of
predictions and expectations (the black hours of 'And more must, in
yet longer light's delay' in 'I wake and feel') to the intuitive 'all day'
timelessness of this in 'Patience, hard thing!':

> Natural heart's ivy, Patience masks
> Our ruins of wrecked past purpose. There she basks
> Purple eyes and seas of liquid leaves all day.

In the ease of 'basking', the richness of 'purple', and the luxuriance of 'seas of liquid leaves' is the very relief Hopkins looks for, and it is sensuous and vernal. There is the same unbidden ease when, at 'unforeseen times', God's smile 'as skies/Betweenpie mountains – lights a lovely mile' ('My own heart let me more have pity on').

In 'Thou art indeed just, Lord' nature is less the restorer than the absolutely contrasting witness against his own condition; '*again*' 'banks and brakes' are laced with flowers, it is '*fresh* wind' that shakes them (my italics), but, now and before, God has left him out of this renewal. Spring is outside him; he does not build, he does not breed: he is other. This is very similar to 'St. Alphonsus Rodriguez', where God's making of mountains and violets and trees is introduced to emphasise the unproductive life of the doorkeeper saint, but the condition Hopkins always sought was that of Holywell, about which he wrote in his Journal:

The strong unfailing flow of the water and the chain of cures from year to year all these centuries took hold of my mind with wonder at the bounty of God in one of His saints, the sensible thing so naturally and gracefully uttering the spiritual reason of its being...and the spring in place leading back the thoughts by its spring in time to its spring in eternity: even now the stress and buoyancy and abundance of the water is before my eyes[21]

Hopkins' wonder was lifelong, for, twelve years after this entry, he was still working on a play called *St. Winefred's Well*, in the event unfinished. The last broken sentence expresses more explicitly than anything else Hopkins wrote the central confidence of his feeling for nature:

As sure as what is most sure,' sure as that spring primroses
Shall new-dapple next year,' sure as to-morrow morning,
Amongst come-back-again things,' things with a revival, things with a recovery,
Thy name...

Nature is there to satisfy the deep hunger for all that life truly is: intuitive not calculated, free of anxiety, creative, vital. The simple happiness of cyclic waking and sleeping is given in the superb 'Moonrise' in 'leaf and leaf', 'eyelid and eyelid', as morning and night are conflated in the midsummer experience so gentle in its nature that the hardness of all categories dissolves. Life has the quiet peacefulness of slumber, and slumber itself the fullness of waking.

I awoke in the Midsummer not-to-call night,¹ in the white and the walk of the
    morning:
The moon, dwindled and thinned to the fringe¹ of a fingernail held to the candle,
Or paring of paradisaïcal fruit,¹ lovely in waning but lustreless,
Stepped from the stool, drew back from the barrow,¹ of dark Maenefa the
    mountain;

The wonderful airy freedom of the opening line comes in part from
the onward anapaestic pulse that catches us up in the energy of
motion, the 'walk' of the morning, before consciousness can collect
itself to pin the experience at one place in one time. The movement
could become a romp, but it is broken by the arresting consecutive
stresses on 'móon' and 'dwíndled', which act also to fasten attention
on the needed locating-point out there; that is, on the moon which
enables us to make sense of where we are. 'Out there', though, is an
expansion of the possibilities of our own consciousness, the sky
being no more remote than the outer limit of the body, 'the fringe
of a fingernail', near with the nearness of one's own being, 'held' and
intimately investigated. The thinning 'to a fringe' is not only a
matter of observable likeness but an attenuation of that outer world,
ordinarily distinct from the private world of the observing consciousness, to the point where the resistance of *things* disappears in
harmony – paradisiacal fruit indeed.

To be attracted to such a life was in Hopkins' view to be drawn
back to primal innocence, to things-before-they-went-wrong, to
sinlessness, to the fundamental order of growth and beauty which
had subsequently been interfered with, bringing in death, decay,
and sterility. To realise in his nature poetry, whatever its limitations
and imperfections, the power of his hunger for that primal order was
one of Hopkins' major artistic achievements. When the hunger was
unrequited, the desire complicated and frustrated, Hopkins' poetry
burst the limits within which it had so often operated previously and
became truly great.

In fact being unwell I was quite downcast: nature in all her parcels and faculties
gaped and fell apart, *fatiscebat*, like a clod cleaving and holding only by strings
of root.²²

It is with such a breaking, such a tenuous, such a precarious holding
to any kind of order (here expressed in a Journal entry written in
1873 while Hopkins was still in training) that we shall be concerned

in Hopkins' great Irish poems. Already, however, some signs have shown themselves of what such a breaking would involve: the strenuousness of his religious conviction, the solitariness of his very genius, the intensity of his love of England, and the ardour of his desire for excellence were all elements which acted to focus upon the ultimate aloneness of his self his full and wrought attention.

5

The cavernous dark

Well! we are all *condamnés*, as Victor Hugo says: we are all under sentence of death but with a sort of indefinite reprieve[1]

Death is the change to end changes; it is both certain and unsettling. This double nature causes the shifts in mood which are evident in Hopkins' poetry and accounts for the ambivalence in him which will become apparent in this chapter.

That polarity in Hopkins of spring and death which I have referred to in chapter 4 is seen in the poem of the same title and brought to its most moving expression in the fine 'Spring and Fall'. In the later poem a little girl in the spring of her life senses the contrary earthward pull of autumn, season of decline, death, and rotting. This is a paradigm of man's condition, for the spring of her life is also the season of utter innocence, the innocence of un-knowingness which is destroyed when the contrariety of experience makes it possible for her to recognise the fact of that innocence by putting a name to it: not until she knows what she is not will she be able to put into words what she is, and the ability to make that recognition will have finished her innocence. The 'fall' is not the fall only of leaves in autumn, it is the fall of man from grace, caused, according to the Bible, by his theft of moral knowledge. Just as wilfully, Margaret is intent on understanding: she *will* 'know why'. The ambiguity of the italicised '*will*' holds another meaning: Margaret will sorrow whether she chooses to or not, and the nature of that future sorrow she will 'know' only too well. The older, colder-hearted Margaret will weep for the realisation that her condition is that of the leaves, but this the little girl has intuitively grasped already:

> It is the blight man was born for,
> It is Margaret you mourn for

– man was born to grieve, born (again the lines carry two senses) to die. It is the inevitability of the onset of knowledge and its complete inability to affect the equally inevitable fate which makes the poem so poignant. The empirical view of life, which looks to external causes to provide explanations for behaviour, must shrug off as inexplicable the fact of Margaret's disproportionate grieving: she will soon learn better, she will soon acquire the tough good sense that is unmoved even at worlds in ruin. But this acquisition is a mere patina of indifference and is of no help to the essential self. Still Margaret will grieve, and, to understand why this is so, 'Spring and Fall' reaches, with the delicateness of a Wordsworthian intimation, beyond the learnt habits of a time-bound world. Though its wise sadness is unique, its theme of transience is persistent in Hopkins.

As I have said, the same theme is presented – somewhat stagily – in the early 'Spring and Death', where, like the figure from Ingmar Bergman's film *The Seventh Seal*, Death goes methodically and unconcernedly about his business, which is here marking flowers for destruction. The same sense of the blight upon life was, however, more eloquently stated in a Liverpool sermon for 1880:

Therefore all the things we see are made and provided for us, the sun, moon, and other heavenly bodies to light us, warm us, and be measures to us of time; coal and rockoil for artificial light and heat; animals and vegetables for our food and clothing; rain, wind, and snow again to make these bear and yield their tribute to us; water and the juices of plants for our drink; air for our breathing; stone and timber for our lodging; metals for our tools and traffic; the songs of birds, flowers and their smells and colours, fruits and their taste for our enjoyment. And so on: search the whole world and you will find it a million-million fold contrivance of providence planned for our use and patterned for our admiration.

But yet this providence is imperfect, plainly imperfect. The sun shines too long and withers the harvest, the rain is too heavy and rots it or in floods spreading washes it away; the air and water carry in their currents the poison of disease; there are poison plants, venomous snakes and scorpions; the beasts our subjects rebel, not only the bloodthirsty tiger that slaughters yearly its thousands, but even the bull will gore and the stallion bite or strike; at night the moon sometimes has no light to give, at others the clouds darken her; she measures time most strangely and gives us reckonings most difficult to make and never exact enough; the coalpits and oilwells are full of explosions, fires, and outbreaks of

sudden death, the sea of storms and wrecks, the snow has avalanches, the earth
landslips; we contend with cold, want, weakness, hunger, disease, death, and
often we fight a losing battle, never a triumphant one; everything is full of fault,
flaw, imperfection, shortcoming; as many marks as there are of God's wisdom in
providing for us so many marks there may be set against them of more being
needed still, of something having made of this very providence a shattered
frame and a broken web.[2]

Hopkins will not take this further to ask why, but it is clear that the
world presented here is more problematic than the world of the
nature poems. The vexations and disasters accumulated here are not
in any immediate way attributable to man; they are part of the fabric
of things.

If that is so, there is nothing to be done. This, at least, is the point
at which 'The Leaden Echo and the Golden Echo' starts, as it
pursues the line of thought which Hopkins' sermon allows to be
truncated. (The poem was written as a song for his unfinished play
St. Winefred's Well, and perhaps this explains why Hopkins'
attempt to heighten language by emphasising essentials has resulted
in repetitions and the sort of verbal trilling represented by 'is kept
with fonder a care,/Fonder a care kept'.) It deals not in doctrines
but in attitudes. The close, calculating, but ineffectual possessiveness
of the leaden echo is not cancelled or even, in its own terms,
adequately answered by the golden, for there is one thing alone
'Which shackles accidents and bolts up change', and that is the
finality of 'death's worst'. The golden echo works instead to make the
question redundant by proposing willing surrender. Its attitude is
that we do not own what appears to be most ours, have no claim on it,
may sleep at nights, as it were, with unlocked doors because what is
at risk does not belong to us anyway – and, because of that, is not at
risk at all. This is not resignation, it is a sort of courage in the flux,
instead of a timorous holding on to what is most easily grasped. It is
the providential lesson of the lilies of the field and the fall of the
sparrow, expressed in the poem in the perpetual springing of the
seed and the regenerative principle that even 'the mere mould' will
waken life; but it is a lesson which takes us 'yonder' out of the 'tall
sun' which 'shines too long and withers the harvest' and the air
which 'carries the poison of disease'. It takes us also out of the world
visibly charged with the grandeur of God – and that is ominous.

The two attitudes of the echoes – the clutching to what is in decline because it is nearest and most obvious, and the confidence in some underlying eternal truth – are firmly a part of 'The Wreck of the Deutschland', though that poem is plainly more extensive in its treatment of the implications of these two contrasting views. The whole of Part the First is about the 'yes' of the personality to Christ in created nature, of which Hopkins' 'yes' is a particular instance, and which is to be seen again in the implied 'yes' of the tall nun's recognition in Part the Second (stanza 29). Both acknowledge God as lord, and their answers are made to reverberate through the poem as a correct identification of the real nature of existence, a realisation of the way things are. The poem is ostensibly built, then, on the parallel between the two cries; but someone who does not share Hopkins' particular faith is likely to discover a different core, one that insists – unlike Hopkins – on the fact of the wreck as a disaster and sees the strengths and weaknesses of his poem accordingly, for what is so carefully and powerfully worked for in Part the First – the idea that God's loving purpose is so constantly present as to be found even in the activity of destruction – is settled on us in Part the Second as something for our unearned acceptance. Instead of resolving the difficulty involved in seeing love in the hostile processes of the storm, Hopkins tries to win our support at this crux with one remarkable coup, a coup which in point of fact strains our sympathy still further. Discussion of that must wait; suffice it to say here that, for Hopkins, the supreme significance of the wreck is not as a calamity but as a revelation.

He is little concerned with the dealings of man with man; the social fact of the wreck is treated very selectively, and this is plain in the way he virtually ignores what *The Times* reported as central facts: the delay in providing rescue for survivors and the subsequent pillaging of dead bodies by local seamen. Of the first *The Times* said:

It is indisputable that there was no lifeboat at Harwich; that the Deutschland lay beaten by the waves on the Kentish Knock for thirty hours without receiving assistance in any shape, and that for one half that time, at least, the signals of distress were seen and recognised by the Harwich seamen. Can any severity of invective carry more condemnation than is involved in these shameful certainties?[3]

In the same edition (Monday 13 December 1875) a reporter wrote:

Twenty bodies have now been brought into Harwich by the steam-tug. Mr. Guy, the inspector of police here, tells me that, with one exception, not a single valuable was found on the persons of these unfortunate people, and that it was clear their pockets had been turned out and rifled. There were ring-marks on the fingers of women, and of at least one gentleman. The rings themselves had disappeared.[4]

In the context of Hopkins' purpose these become local details (the rifling is not mentioned by him) in what is regarded as an instance of something much larger. He treats the wreck in terms which have the effect of making the particular (the newspaper) account inadequate and yet which, in my view, contain inadequacies of a different kind. His poem is both less than and more than the norm of feeling represented, for example, by what *The Times* had to say. It was his achievement to touch in the course of it the precariousness of our habitual expectation of life, and to realise this as something more than a mere encapsulated item of news or momentary interruption of continuities, to make it the presiding fact.

This much may be shown from the superb eleventh stanza which opens Part the Second, and which parallels in imaginative intensity those which begin Part the First. It is like the morality *Everyman* in its treatment of sudden ending. It commences with, as it were, an actor's declamation. Death himself is hidden, and indeed it is his anonymity which he uses to menace. People will only meet ('find') him once, but all his guises here are violent – age is not one of them:

> 'Some find me a sword; some
>   The flange and the rail; flame,
> Fang, or flood' goes Death on drum,
>   And storms bugle his fame.
> But wé dream we are rooted in earth – Dust!
> Flesh falls within sight of us, we, though our flower the same,
>   Wave with the meadow, forget that there must
> The sour scythe cringe, and the blear share come.

Death is vividly presented in his rodomontade with the drum as we are given the braggart omnipotence of the shape-shifter who can be anywhere in any form. The single struck syllables of 'flame', 'fang', and 'flood' *are* the drumbeats; the grossness of the boastfulness is re-enforced by the blare of 'bugle'. Whoever we may think of him as – he will be anyone who needs a crowd to approve or tremble – he is vulgar, and his vulgarity is evinced in the directness of his boasting, the obviousness of his claims, the crude self-esteem there present: Death's pride in himself is hostile to our life, insensitive to us. Before sword, flange, and rail, before scythe and share – before that metallic onslaught – what real chance do soft flowers and tender flesh have? 'But we' introduces a different voice in the drama, and 'dream' evokes the yielding softness of illusion in contrast to the harshness just presented. It is a dream which dissolves in the contemptuous 'dust' that both crumbles the solid earth in which we suppose ourselves rooted and includes us also in its disintegration – the disintegration of centuries where dust has joined dust. 'Flesh', without even the identity of a collective such as 'people', is like 'dust' in its generality and serves the idea of a lack of independent judgement, a deficiency so marked that the so-obvious fact of the common fate is obtusely ignored and all individuality is lost in the fickleness and waving inconstancy of mere motion.

The inadequacy of this directionless conformity is further caught in stanza 12. There are two perspectives in these early stanzas of Part the Second: that of what is and that of what merely appears to be, the last being that of the comfortable social reality of waving with the meadow, taking no notice because everyone else takes no notice, of two hundred people on a sea-journey but, in fact, about to be wrecked. It is their not knowing, the level of unawareness which that social reality represents, which Hopkins plays on while the matter-of-fact tallying of the ship's roll gives way to the feeling-full 'O Father'.

The sense of a reality which subsumes daily experience in something more real is sustained in the next stanzas in the carefully controlled nuances to be found in the description of the publicly observable circumstances of the wreck – 'the infinite air' 'unkind', the soft, murderous 'smother of sand', the drawing of the 'Dead' ship by night. It is continued in the presentation of Hope with the attributes of an elderly mourner at a funeral, grey-haired, futile, with sombre clothes, where 'trenched' and 'carved' suggest the damage done by the physical assault of misery and, all the while, gruelling exposure to the pounding seas. It is a suggestiveness whose significance is made explicit in 'They fought with God's cold', after which identification God's summary power is laconically recorded in brute shorthand parentheses: 'deck/(Crushed them)', 'water (and drowned them)'. By now, however, there are signs of emotion running awry. The description of the death of the 'handy and brave' rescuer of stanza 16 (not a human being, just a thing of motion – 'the to and fro') is the occasion for exhilaration at the power of the force which caused it:

> What could he do
> With the burl of the fountains of air, buck and the flood of the wave?

It is this exhilaration in power which dominates the stanza that opens the whole poem:

> Thou mastering me
> God! giver of breath and bread;
> World's strand, sway of the sea;
> Lord of living and dead;
> Thou hast bound bones and veins in me, fastened me flesh,
> And after it almost unmade, what with dread,
> Thy doing: and dost thou touch me afresh?
> Over again I feel thy finger and find thee.

Hopkins is dealing with a reality more real than the blood-and-bone reality of matter, but it is one which expresses itself through such facts, not beyond them. This is one of the main doctrinal themes of Part the First; the other is that destruction and creation are complementary. We have this in the specially difficult sixth and seventh stanzas, we have it in the stanza just quoted, and we have it later in what Hopkins has to say about the wreck. In this initial stanza making and unmaking are presented as dual expressions of the fact of ultimate power; living or dead, there is one lord and master. This ultimate fact, in turn, insists on there being constancy in the vicissitudes of experience. 'World's strand, sway of the sea' makes the ultimate order one of both stability (with 'strand' as 'beach') and motion. Simultaneously, the only source of all being is presented as, of course, the only source of all matter: he *is* the substance ('strand') of Creation, he *is* the waves.

The complementary nature of stability and motion (suggestive of the fixity which a thing must have for physical identity and also of the way in which because it is temporal it is subject to change and destruction) is further developed in the superb hourglass image of the fourth stanza, with particular focus on the poet's own physical life:

> I am soft sift
> In an hourglass – at the wall
> Fast, but mined with a motion, a drift,
> And it crowds and it combs to the fall;
> I steady as a water in a well, to a poise, to a pane,
> But roped with, always, all the way down from the tall
> Fells or flanks of the voel, a vein
> Of the gospel proffer, a pressure, a principle, Christ's gift.

As the trickling sands of the hourglass remain stable where they touch its glass wall but move inexorably downwards at the funnel centre, so the life of man is always in perpetual dissolution, the same but changing (from Ireland Hopkins was to write that he was not dying, 'except at the rate that we all are'[5]). The fine consonance in the verb-noun 'soft sift' re-enforces one's sense of mutability; the poet is both material which is confined by its physical being in time and something all the while purposefully proven. The liquid motion suggested by the dribble of sand is sustained in an image which draws on Hopkins' life at Stonyhurst and at St Beuno's: the northern fells and the Welsh mountains supply water to the lowland in a way which shows that, for Hopkins, this physical dissolution is a movement toward not emptiness but equipoise. He is secured by Christ as the 'ropes' of streams secure the valley waters.

Were the passengers on the *Deutschland* so secured? In stanza 12 Hopkins employs the same idea of the rope that he uses in the fourth stanza and also in his meditations (in one note Hopkins speaks of the redemptive effect of the incarnation in these terms: 'A 60-fathom coil of cord running over the cliff's edge round by round...40 fathom already gone and the rest will follow, when a man sets his foot on it and saves both what is hanging and what has not yet stirred to run. Or seven tied by the rope on the Alps; four go headlong, then the fifth, strong as Samson, checks them and the two behind do not even feel the strain').[6] Did 'the million of rounds of thy mercy not reeve even them in?' Hopkins fancies that the cry of the tall nun may have alerted the other passengers to the reality of their situation (stanza 31), for their time of suffering is, in fact, the moment of their inevitable confrontation with God. As we shall see later, he builds on that fancy.

His own confrontation is described in the second and third stanzas of Part the First, which, like the eleventh stanza, involve us in a level of imaginative intensity not present again in Hopkins till the Irish poems. It is an intensity which comes from Hopkins' ability, when he is at his best, to touch feelings which are not, in the verse, rationally organised as an explicit progression of thoughts or obviously identifiable pattern of images, an ability which, inasmuch as it sometimes operates beneath the complex surface of the poetry, might be described as subliminal. It works spatially and is difficult for the critic to indicate without appearing to be merely fanciful or else, by supplying connections which the poet himself does not, either losing the power of the verse in exposition or seeming to suggest that it is the primary pattern, exclusive of the main one, when, in fact, it is rather in the nature of counterpoint – the poetry's buried power. (I have already hinted at its presence in 'Hurrahing in Harvest' in the way that poem is built to create the expectation of and achieve some climactic connection between earth and heaven.) However, it is very distinctive of Hopkins when he is at his most intense, this primitivism: the risks had better be taken.

It is not contentious to say that in the first stanza Hopkins is being handled. He is 'bound', touched, and feels physically. In one form that handling is as of a child who has his coat (of flesh) fastened for him and feels laid on him an admonitory finger. That act provokes in stanza 2 the self-justifying, near-petulant child's retort, 'I did say yes'. This sort of assertiveness is inadequate to the power of adult presence, however, and he is confronted in stanza 3 with a form so large and threatening that the frowning 'face' dominates his consciousness as, by its relative hugeness, it might in a child's perspective. The challenge worked out in these personal terms is a challenge to self-confidence. It is realised physically in the risk of the 'hurtle', the hurtle perhaps of a river in spate or of any object dropped into a chasm (to place its significance narrowly is necessary only for establishing continuity); it is a dangerous gulf to be leapt. The challenge is met in an impulsive 'fling': reason is no help, the body must do it (the Kierkegaardian leap of faith is here a physical test of courage). How natural, after this success, is the rise in self-esteem, the elation at something satisfactorily accomplished, the spiring upward movement of the verse, 'bold to boast', flashing and towering.

But such a pattern of growth in self-confidence is beneath, if not actually at odds with, the explicit statement of these stanzas with their reliance on *God*'s mercy. To that main statement I now return.

Though stanza 2 speaks of 'the walls, altar and hour and night', of the 'midriff astrain' with hours of kneeling prayer, the fear of God so occupies the centre of the poet's attention that we begin to lose any sense of the external world. What is happening is preternatural, apocalyptic; God is a physical adversary of enormous size and speed, knowing as well as the poet knows

> The swoon of a heart that the sweep and the hurl of thee trod
> Hard down with a horror of height.

In these stanzas the similarities with the Irish sonnets of desolation are marked (especially with 'Carrion Comfort' and 'No worst, there is none'). The poet is caught by his opponent at the edge of things, desperate (and – using, with what different result, the same device he employs less happily in 'The Leaden Echo and the Golden Echo' – the broken syntax breathlessly shows the desperation) for a place of security:

> The frown of his face
> Before me, the hurtle of hell
> Behind, where, where was a, where was a place?

At that time ('that spell') he turned instinctively, 'carrier-witted', to the Eucharist, central to his faith. Thus he escaped from the fire of hell to the Pentecostal flame of the Holy Spirit, rose from one level of God's approval to another (so I read the third stanza's obscure last line).

In the opening stanza of the poem, which, as J. E. Keating points out,[7] draws on the Book of Job, God is 'mastering' and dreadful; in the second he causes terror and swooning; then, suddenly from the unbearable mental pressure in the imminence of 'hurtle' and 'horror of height' there is a change of state which is not rescue but release. Instead of the big gulf there is a free winging through air in the spontaneous power of 'whirled' and 'fling' and the surging access of strength in 'tower': the crisis is passed; the relief prefigures the easy graciousness of stanza 5. What has been worked out privately here in a psychic drama will be worked out publicly in the disaster of Part the Second; the five stanzas which close Part the First work to establish the necessary connection as God is urged to 'Wring... Man's malice, with wrecking and storm'.

These five stanzas also go some way to account (though, as I see the matter, not sufficiently) for the way Hopkins ultimately treats the predicament of the passengers and crew. Stanzas 6 and 7 follow Scotus in saying that Christ's incarnation is central in God's communication with man because it is the fulfilment of God's creative purpose and only secondarily a redemptive act. In the way we customarily use language, Hopkins says in stanza 8, we save the most powerful word (be it a good or a bad one) till last; so Christ, Creation's most powerful expression, is Creation's culmination. He is also the same sort of dual expression – of God's activity in making and destroying – that we have already had in the poem's first stanza. Christ was born, but to be destroyed on the cross. As in his letter about Bridges' sister, Mrs Plow, Hopkins is maintaining that God's destruction is loving. But there is more in stanza 7 than the complacency in doctrine that we have in that letter. 'Warm-laid grave' turns Christ's birth into a death-in-time; 'womb-life grey' makes the whole of Christ's life a pregnancy, a 'swelling to be' – a paradox indeed, for such 'being' is the seeming not-being of the crucifixion, the death moment actually the moment of birth fulfilling the expectation that is the very nature of pregnancy, its looking-forward-ness. More than this, the conflations of the poetry are such that the urgent wish for release of all passion-full moments – of coitus, of birth-labour, of violent dying – 'dense and driven', is evoked in these lines as resulting in achievement, the buoyant 'high flood' that approves being as a full thing, and not as drab or dull or vacant or finite.

The full significance of what Hopkins says in stanzas 6 and 7 might be blurred by a reader and made no different from traditional Christian theology, but, in fact, Hopkins has fenced it with warnings to avoid that: 'few know this', 'here the faithful waver', 'What none would have known of it'. Not only does the 'stress' of God's beauty in nature (which he has written about in stanza 5) not have some distant origin as an intervention in ordinary life, but suffering is not determined by God as an interruption either – neither is a remote, occasional decision. The beauty and chastisement which 'stars and storms deliver' 'rides time like riding a river': it is part of the very fabric of Creation as the will of God. This has been so since the incarnation, the completion of Creation ('It dates from day/Of his going in Galilee'); Galilee and Calvary, birth and death, are conflated because, although apparently contradictory, they are the twin elements in God's single purpose. Christ's life is considered as one act, as one moment when God, *in propria persona* as it were, entered time. He had been felt before and is 'in high flood yet', but that was the explicit moment. As such, since it included the Passion, it is representative of the ambiguity of life – birth for death.

The wreck of the *Deutschland* also has such a meaning, but, as I hope to show a little later, it is Hopkins' attempt to find a creative purpose in the destruction it involved which spoils the later stanzas of this poem. At the moment it simply needs to be recognised that Hopkins is preparing for that attempt by writing about Christ as the finest expression of God's creativity, and it can be seen how easily the theological explanation follows on from stanza 5, where Christ is in the stars and the thunder and the sunset. Thus, in stanza 8, men feel intuitively what Hopkins has just been speaking about (in keeping with Scotus, Hopkins had come to believe that man's unbidden nature turned like a homing bird to the source of its being). They worship Christ instinctively, 'Never ask if meaning it, wanting it, warned of it – men go', and this is the ground for the paradoxes of stanza 9, for, if Christ is in nature, he is in the storm as well as the stars, is working creatively and redemptively in the wreck.

> Thou art lightning and love, I found it, a winter and warm;
> Father and fondler of heart thou hast wrung:

– Hopkins can say from his own experience that, when God's dark descends, he is 'most...merciful then'.

Part the First is, then, rigorously logical; every stanza develops the idea of the double nature of experience, of making and unmaking, of fixity and change, of birth and death, and no stanzas more so than those which insist on this duality even in the central fact of the incarnation: that God's best making was destroyed also. What is there in Part the Second to warrant this introduction with its emphasis on the incarnation? A diffuse feeling that, even in storm and suffering, God's purposes are benign? No; something more specific than this – and here we come to the coup I wrote of earlier, Hopkins' attempt to carry us with him in his view that there is creative love and redemption in pain and misery. In her *The Dragon in the Gate* Professor Schneider makes the striking and original claim that Hopkins is saying, particularly in stanza 28, 'that a miracle had occurred, that during the night of terror at sea Christ had appeared to the nun, not in a subjective or imagined vision but as a real miraculous presence and that this event, once acknowledged and published to the world, might become the needed signal, the turning point for the conversion of English Christians'. Her argument directs attention to the facts that Hopkins speaks of Christ as '*Ipse*' (his very self) with its very particular association 'because of its prominence in the Mass, at the minor elevation', that he spends time rejecting other possible meanings for the tall nun's call, that he several times uses the word 'fetch' which is, in much of the north and west of England, 'a name for an apparition, wraith, ghost, or spirit, sometimes of the living, sometimes of the dead', and which Hopkins himself used when distinguishing between a subjective vision and a miracle, and that this reading explains Hopkins' wish that not every part of the poem should be quite clear.[8] To my knowledge her idea has not been warmly received; there are some apparent difficulties in the way of its acceptance, but it seems to me that she is right. The teaching about the incarnation in Part the First is there to provide for what is, in effect, another incarnation in Part the Second, one which is there as justifying, by the fact of its happening, pain and loss. Its importance to us is that it is the offered evidence – visible evidence – of redemptiveness and loving-kindness otherwise indiscernible in the cold, black waters and the flakes of snow.

We should set aside Elizabeth Schneider's idea that the miracle, once publicised, would be 'the needed signal' for conversion, because this is at odds with her recognition that the obscurity which surrounds its announcement in the poem accords with Hopkins' 'indeed I was not over-desirous that the meaning of all should be quite clear, at least unmistakeable': much-needed signals are of little value if they are deliberately obscure. However, the rest of what she says seems to me to represent a very considerable new insight into what is happening in the poem – and the miracle is not simply an illustration of a more general position, it is the particular focus of that position, the substance of the poem. The reference which Elizabeth Schneider gives to Hopkins' devotional use of 'fetch' ('I suppose the vision of the pregnant woman to have been no mere vision but the real fetching, presentment, or "adduction" of the persons, Christ and Mary, themselves')[9] is powerful on its own, but the way the crucial stanza is constructed seems to me conclusive. There are a number of difficulties for it to overcome: if Hopkins were proclaiming a miraculous appearance rather than something the nun alone saw, or believed she saw, the appearance would have to be public and shared, yet there seems to be no other voice in the poem, apart from the tall nun's, recognising Christ; moreover, Hopkins stresses that she was unique in reading 'the unshapeable shock night'. After a story whose narrative progress has been impeded by pieces of discarded speculation about the real meaning of the nun's cry, the obstacles are overcome thus:

> But how shall I...make me room there:
> Reach me a...Fancy, come faster –
> Strike you the sight of it? look at it loom there,
> Thing that she...There then! the Master,
> *Ipse*, the only one, Christ, King, Head:
> He was to cure the extremity where he had cast her;
> Do, deal, lord it with living and dead;
> Let him ride, her pride, in his triumph, despatch and have done with
> his doom there.

There is meaning in the fragments of sentences which form the first half of the stanza. The first voice is Hopkins', wondering how to go about the problem he was left with at the end of the previous stanza, namely that of showing what the nun's cry really meant. The next voice is on board ship, of someone elbowing through a crowd to see – or, more probably (in view of the purposefulness indicated by the colon and the verb following), to do – something.

The poet's position is now little better than that of the one on board
ship: he cannot understand what is happening and thus – my most
tentative suggestion – invokes the aid of the imagination. 'Strike you
the sight of it?' takes us back on board ship where we are watching
some apparition, unidentified but visible – 'it' looms – and, moreover, the 'thing' that 'she', the nun, has some particular relation
with, the thing that she called out to. Now the truth is realised and
spoken in the poem, but still not by the others on ship who are left
with their unrecognised spectre-shape, the existence of which has
been publicly acknowledged as a fact quite separate from the nun: he
was Christ, and – lest there be any mistake amongst those who *have*
understood this – his very self, not an image in the mind but 'the
only one'. His personal appearance is further indicated by the way in
which a purpose is then ascribed to him, independent of the nun:
'He was to cure the extremity where he had cast her'. It could be
argued that 'Fancy, come faster' is the nun's wish for a clearer vision
of what she has so far but dimly conceived in her mind, but this has
to be rejected because of the clear separation indicated in 'thing that
she' and the way in which the appearance is twice located 'there',
away from her. (The cry might also be a parallel to 'O Christ, Christ,
come quickly' of stanza 24, in which case 'Fancy' would mean 'that
which I have desired'.)

It was Peter who saw Christ when, in the gospel story, his lord
walked on the water, and it was he who had the confidence to try to
join him. So, as Professor Schneider points out, the reference to the
nun as a 'Simon Peter of a soul' in the stanza immediately following
Christ's appearance is particularly pointed. Stanzas 32 and 33, she
shows, are a recapitulation of what has been revealed about the
essential nature of the storm; they finish, again, with Christ walking
on the water, 'fetched in the storm of his strides'. The poem is
improved by a reading which acknowledges that Hopkins is speaking
of a miracle in stanza 28, in that it is seen as more tightly worked;
but it is not redeemed. Now, instead of 'The dense and the driven
Passion' as the connecting-point with Hopkins' faith, we are given
a *deus ex machina*.

Is the problem the one of the great divide between those who
accept the existence of the supernatural and those who deny it? I

think not. It does, of course, matter whether the explicit source of proffered help in the poem – the 'cure' for the extremity - is real or illusory, for the miracle is to be taken by us as a sign of the compassion operating even in the storm, but that is not the decisive issue. What counts is that, adroitly handled though it may be, the divine intervention is but one mark of Hopkins' circumventing the intransigences of human experience. However strong one's faith, snow is not the less numbing, nor wind-lashed water less salt and blinding. Physical substances have their properties still, but Hopkins moves further and further away from them into pietist reveries of his own. The poem is, in Dr Leavis' words, 'a great poem – at least for the first two-thirds of it',[10] and what happens in the final third (or more) is that Hopkins has lost the sense of a *wreck*. The problems the disaster poses, and which till now have been so determinedly faced, are abandoned for pat answers.

This shows in the overturn of normal values which we find in stanza 21, where God is approved as hunter, and where the snowstorm becomes, as it were, a sort of baroque art-work or a bounty of petals:

> but thou art above, thou Orion of light;
> Thy unchancelling poising palms were weighing the worth,
> Thou martyr-master: in thy sight
> Storm flakes were scroll-leaved flowers, lily showers – sweet heaven was astrew in them.

It shows, too, in the canvassed notion that the wreck might be a harvest (stanza 31). Those non-Catholics who died in the storm were 'not uncomforted' because the cry of the tall nun was as a bell which could ring the news of 'lovely-felicitous Providence' and

> Startle the poor sheep back! is the shipwreck then a harvest, does tempest carry the grain for thee?

The idea of men as a flock of sheep is a Biblical one and hence unoriginal, but in other places Hopkins had considerable success in reworking Biblical imagery. What goes wrong here is easier to see if this image is taken in conjunction with the one that follows, one of harvest, again Biblical and again expressive of God's care. As the shepherd looks after his flock, so the lord gathers into his barn. But the images are badly used in the poem. The sheep of the Bible who need the shepherd's care become sheep who can be driven at will,

'startled...back'. They are not so much helpless as fickle. Furthermore, the grain, which in the Bible is separated from the chaff and
stored protectively, here becomes an index of gain, a harvest which
seems to make God benefit at others' expense. The Biblical tones are
changed for ones which suit the poem's praise of God's power, but at
the expense of their original compassion.

The formalism of the last fourteen stanzas (the trouble really
begins in stanza 22, though exception might also be taken to the
sectarianism of stanza 20) is another debilitating feature. The
number of drowned nuns is in itself of no human significance, but
Hopkins makes it important as the number of Christ's wounds:

> Five! the finding and sake
> And cipher of suffering Christ.

The implication is that the exiled nuns are chosen for death in this
way, and it is supported by the otherwise irrelevant apostrophe to
St Francis, St Francis' stigmata being taken as an illustration of the
fact that Christ marks men out for sacrifice, 'But he scores it in
scarlet himself on his own bespoken'. The effect of these stanzas
(22 and 23) is to give the disaster a ritual significance which further
distances the poem from the reader who does not share Hopkins'
preoccupation. Again the verse is weak. The ugliness of 'seal of his
seraph-arrival!' is followed by

> and these thy daughters
> And five-livèd and leavèd favour and pride,
> Are sisterly sealed in wild waters,
> To bathe in his fall-gold mercies, to breathe in his all-fire glances.

There is an uneasy juxtaposition here of the physical plight of the
nuns and the spiritual reality which Hopkins sees underlying it. Fire
and water are inimical, yet he puts them together here, and the ideas
of bathing in 'mercies' and breathing in 'glances' are strained (in
these 'wild waters', cruelly, the nuns are *not* 'bathing').

The poem recovers in stanza 24 when it returns to the nuns'
predicament, contrasted with the poet's ease:

> Away in the loveable west,
> On a pastoral forehead of Wales,
> I was under a roof here, I was at rest,
> And they the prey of the gales;

and the recovery is essentially one of human sympathy. It is temporary. No amount of explanation can entirely take away the morbidity of the stanza which follows (where Hopkins is asking the Holy Spirit to aid him in interpreting the meaning of the nun's cry):

> The majesty! what did she mean?
> Breathe, arch and original Breath.
> Is it love in her of the being as her lover had been?
> Breathe, body of lovely Death.

Again, as in the stanza about 'scroll-leaved flowers', we are aware of the mistaken aesthetic: Death is beautiful; how remote from 'flame, Fang, or flood'! By this point in the poem we are left either recoiling from feelings such as these or such clumsiness as the consonant chime which closes the stanza ('The keener to come at the comfort for feeling the combating keen?'), or welcoming such occasional felicities as 'the moth-soft Milky Way', where moth-time is suitably evoked in the visual attractions of the night sky (the apt term, *synaesthesia*, is a cumbersome word for applauding this delicate example of Hopkins' essential tactile quality, but it is that). The vital hold has gone.

The cause of the damage to the poem lies in the fact that the imaginative grip which Hopkins has on reality, present and ultimate, is abandoned in a crude and unsatisfactory exchange: spinning snow is now flowers, Death is lovely, the old problem of why a loving God should permit suffering is no longer being seriously acknowledged in the poem because the terms in which its last third is written forget that suffering was ever that at all. Moreover, we are no longer dealing with a God who is dynamically in the fabric of life, we are dealing with substitute statuary. The Christ who appears to the nun does not say or do anything, he merely 'looms'. How could one feel any reverence for such a 'thing'? He utters nothing, he makes no movement; his presence there is of as little consequence as it is when, later in the poem, a similar statuesque form appears ('past all/Grasp God, throned behind/Death'). In the last four stanzas God, Christ, Mary, and the now-blessed nuns are sufficiently evoked to make us feel that we are looking at a set piece; beyond this in any direction, emotionally, intellectually, or spiritually, we may not go; in more than the obvious sense, the poem has come to a stop.

The wreck of the *Deutschland* was a large subject for a powerful imagination, and Hopkins shows a confidence there in the happy justice of life which was subsequently to decline. Great decisions and great sacrifices were congenial to Hopkins' mind, but littlenesses wore him down, and his poetry shows increasingly a hiatus between the idealistic level on which his mind customarily worked and the small practical application of his convictions to the complexities of life. His beliefs did not change but his confidence shrank. Increasingly he held his convictions in the face of a puzzling and a growing darkness.

A part of 'The Wreck of the Deutschland' disappoints; nonetheless, the poem is by virtue of the achieved depth of so many of its stanzas an important accomplishment. It was easier for Hopkins to meet the challenges posed by the maritime disaster, however, than for him to deal adequately with life's quiet, bed-ridden seeping away. 'Felix Randal', his sole attempt at writing of the personal experience of death, does not manage to escape - try as it does - from its tendency to be quite the opposite of personal, a matter of role and type (the role being Hopkins' priestly one, and the type that of strong maleness).

There is another poem within 'Felix Randal', struggling to get out from the public shell of this one where 'ah well' in its safe, sighing generality substitutes for, and protects - in the way it cloaks inadequacy - any revealing of the tender, touched self. The existence of that private self in the confusion and depth of its feeling is evident in the first tercet (the poem is similar to 'The Lantern out of Doors' in its move to supplant the glib and complacent); but Hopkins is unable to deal with the human complexity of the estranging fact of sickness, implicitly demanding how those in good health can ever adequately minister to those who are not. He turns aside from this, the real crux of the poem, and celebrates the farrier in the full vigour of his health. Felix has fussed, become incoherent, lost patience, cursed, and seemed to present himself for once in Hopkins' verse as something other than a fine-featured hero (though handsome he is) or an obdurate wrecker of God's world. Then we have this:

> How far from then forethought of, all thy more boisterous years,
> When thou at the random grim forge, powerful amidst peers,
> Didst fettle for the great grey drayhorse his bright and battering sandal!

In the power lies Felix's attraction for Hopkins; and in the powerlessness of sickness lies the felt core of the poem, away from which Hopkins has been drawn by his characteristic preference for vigour. It was a Roman practice to put sandals on horses' hooves: the detail is a further indication of Hopkins' movement away from the complex ordinariness of a Lancashire blacksmith's death.

In 'The Wreck of the Deutschland' and 'Felix Randal' – and also in the lightweight 'The Loss of the Eurydice' – Hopkins is involved with the deaths of particular people: there are circumstances to shape his response in each case. However, for the general question of transience to which he periodically returns there are no such local guides and, in their absence, the recurrent motif he employs is of black night against which are set remote stars, brief sparks, vanishing lights. The 'womb-of-all, home-of-all, hearse-of-all night' ('Spelt from Sibyl's Leaves') represents the unknowable mystery of existence outside the self ('self' here being representative of all human 'selves'), the self which is the core of individual consciousness. Into that night he will himself pass with equanimity, but, inasmuch as it represents the fate of all visible life, it seems to emphasise the ultimate aloneness of all selves (this is true, I think, even of 'Spelt from Sibyl's Leaves', where the awesomeness of the mystery which surrounds us is described in terms of consequences that are personal).

Such equanimity shows in an early (September 1864) fragment:

> – I am like a slip of comet,
> Scarce worth discovery, in some corner seen
> Bridging the slender difference of two stars,
> Come out of space, or suddenly engender'd
> By heady elements, for no man knows:
> But when she sights the sun she grows and sizes
> And spins her skirts out, while her central star
> Shakes its cocooning mists; and so she comes
> To fields of light; millions of travelling rays
> Pierce her; she hangs upon the flame-cased sun,
> And sucks the light as full as Gideon's fleece:
> But then her tether calls her; she falls off,
> And as she dwindles shreds her smock of gold
> Amidst the sistering planets, till she comes
> To single Saturn, last and solitary;
> And then goes out into the cavernous dark.

So I go out: my little sweet is done:
I have drawn heat from this contagious sun:
To not ungentle death now forth I run.

'Not ungentle death' presents itself here as meeting the same psychic need which 'Heaven-Haven' and 'The Habit of Perfection' answer monastically, the need for repose (here, in relief from a life which exhausts by its intensity). 'The cavernous dark' is the final, fixed reality on which a swift, brilliant existence has no effect, except the more to point by contrast that the dumb, black, interstellar spaces are silent and empty still. In a moment of particular desolation in 1866 Hopkins had written (in 'Nondum') that 'Vacant creation's lamps appal', but it was not his own fate which caused such a shudder of loneliness but a feeling of the ultimate inaccessibility of others' lives and deaths. 'The cavernous dark' seemed to confirm that we are finally isolated, denied communion one with another.

When the supporting evidence of the senses is removed there is, for Hopkins, faith, a promise, to cope with the unknown. Both 'The Lantern out of Doors' (1877) and 'That Nature is a Heraclitean Fire and of the comfort of the Resurrection' (1888) seek to deal with absence, to reach out beyond the visible and go into the blackness. In each case the movement of the poem is of one experience being supplanted by another: except as a promise, the then does not touch the now (unlike the opening stanzas of 'The Wreck of the Deutschland' where the two are inseparable); the reader, whatever his faith, is left with an enigma.

In the earlier poem the blackness has become inhospitable, as difficult to penetrate as turbid water or foggy marsh gloom (the consonantal difficulty which clogs utterance at this point in the poem enacts the resistance of the air). Exceptional people beat it back, temporarily, then are lost to sight. 'Out of sight is out of mind', says Hopkins, in a cliché the inadequacy of which the poem's mere existence demonstrates. However, the answering reassurance that 'Christ minds' does not cancel the blackness, for it exists in another dimension.

The same is true of 'That Nature is a Heraclitean Fire and of the comfort of the Resurrection', which is cleft in two by 'Enough! the Resurrection', and where the conjunction in the title is a sign that in this case we are again dealing with two distinctly different experiences. The fire which burns endlessly in nature goes out in man, whose ultimate destiny is of a different order from that known here and now. The poem's opening is light-hearted enough. Nature is, as in the poems Hopkins wrote in Wales (this one was written in Ireland), celebrated in its activity and change, but it is not the impetuous, ecstatic celebration of 'Look at the stars!' The busy preoccupation of nature in the Welsh sonnets is here a point of contrast. Nature burns – and that with a brightness carried into the exorbitance of the language in words such as 'shivelights' and 'shadowtackle' and in marked alliterative patterns ('long lashes lace, lance') – but nature is renewed; for man, renewal scarcely seems possible:

> But quench her bonniest, dearest' to her, her clearest-selvèd spark
> Man, how fast his firedint,' his mark on mind, is gone!
> Both are in an unfathomable, all is in an enormous dark
> Drowned.

Man dies into something beyond his understanding, but even the fact that he has ever been is displaced from consciousness. 'Death blots black out', 'We have an interval, and then our place knows us no more'[11] – in this poem how close Hopkins' feeling of transience comes to Pater's precarious brevity, for there is nothing in the world of sense to keep metaphysics warm. There is no trace of man that will bear witness to his distinctiveness, what he is is lost in space and time,

> nor mark
> Is any of him at all so stark
> But vastness blurs and time' beats level.

This is Pater's 'inevitable shipwreck';[12] it is also Hopkins' – then

> Across my foundering deck shone
> A beacon, an eternal beam.

The second coda to the sonnet opens out the theme of 'the comfort of the Resurrection', but it is a comfort despite the natural course of earthly life, not as part of it. Though man perishes in the world, 'leave but ash', yet he persists. The ash of the pyre becomes carbon in its most imperishable form – but only after the burning:

This Jack, joke, poor potsherd,¹ patch, matchwood, immortal diamond,
    Is immortal diamond.

The incarnation (Christ 'was what I am') is the essential connection
between now and then, but its light in this poem is powerless to
help the understanding, or to irradiate life: no meaning is worked
out between the glittering immortality which the poet presents as
man's ultimate spiritual destiny and the intervening blackness
which, in time, separates him from it.

If the nobility of man has shrunk in this poem to the point where
man is a 'joke', then common 'Jack' is to be pitied for his littleness
in the face of the enormous unknown which surrounds him. In 'The
shepherd's brow' Hopkins stops only a little way short of despising
him. However, it is to be disputed whether the poem is what
Bridges found it when he wrote, 'this must have been thrown off one
day in a cynical mood, which he could not have wished permanently
to intrude among his last serious poems'.¹³ It was not fitful, but part
of the oscillation in his view of man (an oscillation which also
includes 'world's loveliest') – as Hopkins' editors point out,¹⁴ he
made five full drafts of it so it was obviously considered. Cynicism
there is (not all wives are 'hussies'), but the poem moves beyond
this. Hopkins opens out new possibilities for his work in realising
that the truth is not necessarily a choice between opposites, but may
involve a change of modes. As Swift read lessons for us in contracted
or exaggerated images of man, so Hopkins looks in reflections (on
the 'brow', in the 'smooth spoons') to find a true perspective:

> The shepherd's brow, fronting forked lightning, owns
> The horror and the havoc and the glory
> Of it. Angels fall, they are towers, from heaven – a story
> Of just, majestical, and giant groans.
> But man – we, scaffold of score brittle bones;
> Who breathe, from groundlong babyhood to hoary
> Age gasp; whose breath is our *memento mori* –
> What bass is *our* viol for tragic tones?
> He! Hand to mouth he lives, and voids with shame;
> And, blazoned in however bold the name,
> Man Jack the man is, just; his mate a hussy.
> And I that die these deaths, that feed this flame,
> That...in smooth spoons spy life's masque mirrored: tame
> My tempests there, my fire and fever fussy.

The spectacle of a man watching sheep and thus exposed to the elements is itself an acknowledgement of a power represented by the lightning flickering across his forehead, and the same power is involved in the clash of God and the angels of Lucifer – its very scale makes it majestic. But, in contrast, man, insubstantial, in bondage to his breath, is mortal like every other man jack, has a body common in its processes. (As in 'The Blessed Virgin compared to the Air we Breathe', he has 'the deathdance in his blood'.) But, if life is too mean to be tragic, tragic emotion is out of place also: seen in perspective the poet's own passions – Hopkins realises – are, really, miniature; they are not grand but fussy; histrionics – it now appears – in a spoon.

In his poem Hopkins' primitivism once more shows itself, chiefly in the spatial movement which underpins the thought and re-enforces the pattern of values. When angels fall, it is with the full weight of, and from the full height of, towers. Man's 'scaffold' is a secondary thing, and it lacks the dignity and the weight which the lofty angel-buildings have. These can fall – and their doing so is the most immediate reason for the resulting heavy 'giant groans' – because they are high enough to be in jeopardy, but man does not fall in the poem because he anyway exists at the base 'groundlong' level where the angels finish up. He is meanly safe from plummeting, not at tragic risk. Only the letters in his name are high; his aspirations are pretensions, he does not actually become tragically exposed by trying to achieve what is above him. If that is so, says Hopkins, it is foolish to consume oneself in burning zeal or resentment at it – the fervour is ill-proportioned, physically out of scale. But such a tempering conformity to a destiny conceived of in such low terms is, of course, an expression of final bitterness that it should be so.

That element in Hopkins' work which begins in 'The Wreck of the Deutschland' with a celebration of God's power ends – with entirely consistent logic – in 'The shepherd's brow' as a record of man's impotence. In this sense the poem shares a common theme with the two others Hopkins wrote in the last months of his life, though the impotence which they describe is Hopkins' own, a felt failure in creativeness expressed in sexual terms. 'The shepherd's brow' makes life a dismal, inglorious holding on, and its explicit

concern with the *memento mori* places it in this chapter rather than
the next. However, I suspect it has a common origin with those
sonnets which come from the clash between his complete determination to live a full and useful life in the service of his faith and the
overburdening work which he came to see as the near-complete
frustration of that aim. Hopkins' strong sense that the world has
forms through which God's meaning is discoverable is scarcely
evident in his Irish writings (his inner world is one where *he* makes
such forms as there are), as he becomes involved in a complex
dialectic between suffering and justice. 'The Wreck of the Deutschland' leads on, not to the nature poems composed in sequence, but
to the dark sonnets which are amongst his greatest.

6

Ireland

It is as if one were dazzled by a spark or star in the dark,
seeing it but not seeing by it.[1]

The poems Hopkins wrote in the last five and a half years of his life
are often of such an intimate nature that one is encouraged to believe
that they reveal some hitherto concealed but essential truth about
him. Here latent conflicts are made actual, here facts previously
obscured are made available for examination (so one might suppose):
this is the place to begin. (Hence the mistaken advice that 'The
Windhover' is 'best approached retrospectively from the standpoint
of the later sonnets'.[2]) However, such beginnings are never genuine;
of necessity they are always influenced by judgements – sometimes,
by assumptions – about Hopkins' earlier years. The poems so often
describe a condition of life rather than its immediate causes that the
assumptions can, with some show of plausibility, be advanced *as*
causes. (Thus it is suggested that 'In constantly denying and rejecting
the artist in himself he was rejecting his true self...and it finally
caught up with him in the last years in Dublin.'[3]) This has the
effect of giving to the poems a certain specialism (only a priest who
should really have given his life to poetry would write like this, it is
implied), and those who see Hopkins' whole life as a specialism (the
priesthood) do not dissent from this, they simply locate the specialist
interest in a different place (only a religious could write like this,
the experience these poems treat derives from the seminary'). To
claim back the poetry from specialisms is the chief purpose of this
chapter.

Hopkins was appointed to the Chair of Greek in the Royal

University of Ireland early in 1884. The job mainly involved the
management of examinations, and from the first Hopkins did not
want it. He was to write later that the 'resolution of the senate of the
R. U. came to me, inconvenient and painful';[4] at the time, he told
Newman, tactfully (the University was Newman's own attempt to
provide for Catholic higher education in Ireland), that he had tried
to decline the offer, feeling unfitted for the position.[5] Such misgivings as Hopkins had were only deepened when he took up his post.
No amount of money, he thought, could be suitable repayment for
the six examinations he had to conduct every year;[6] the post was 'an
honour and an opening and has many bright sides, but at present it
has also some dark ones and this in particular that I am not at all
strong, not strong enough for the requirements, and do not see at all
how I am to become so'.[7] His anxiety about being too weak to bear
the responsibilities of the job was swiftly justified. Two months
later he was telling Bridges, 'I am, I believe, recovering from a deep
fit of nervous prostration (I suppose I ought to call it): I did not
know but I was dying',[8] and in July 1884 Dixon wrote to him saying
that he was distressed 'by the news of your illness, or at least
prostration of strength'.[9] In August Hopkins was 'the better and
fresher for my holiday',[10] but in October with 557 scripts on hand
('let those who have been thro' the like say what that means') he was
again 'drowned' in examinations,[11] and the situation worsened
during the first half of 1885. He had unwisely refused an invitation
to spend Christmas with his parents,[12] on the grounds that winter
travelling would tax him and that it would not look well if he returned
to England having been so short a time in Ireland. He regretted the
decision.[13] By April he was talking of himself as living in a 'coffin of
weakness and dejection',[14] and in May he thought this dejection
resembled insanity.[15] In the spring and summer of that year his
misery reached its intensest pitch; then in August he went on holiday
to his parents at Hampstead and to Patmore at Hastings and
temporarily recovered.[16] This pattern of cumulative dejection
relieved by holidays, particularly those away from Ireland, was
repeated in following years, though the dejection was less severe.
In 1886 he recovered his spirits in a fortnight's holiday in Wales,[17]
and in 1887 in a visit to his parents and to Bridges;[18] but in 1888 a

not entirely successful stay in Scotland was scarcely adequate.[19] 'All I really need is a certain degree of relief and change',[20] he had decided, but he doubted whether he could last long in this sort of life. He did not repeat what seems to have been the mistake in 1884 of staying in Ireland the whole year through, but though this was sufficient to keep the misery in check it did not end it.

Hopkins – who was physically not strong – found his work onerous, then, and it made him wretched. However – and this is of great importance – he also thought that there was little value in it. In 1887 he tells Bridges, 'Tomorrow morning I shall have been three years in Ireland, three hard wearying wasting wasted years'[21] (it should be remembered that Hopkins is telling this to a man who has a deep dislike of the Society of Jesus, and that his own pride would normally have prevented him from making such an admission), and in 1888 he gives his mother this considered view of his life.

I am now working at examination-papers all day and this work began last month and will outlast this one. It is great, very great drudgery. I can not of course say it is wholly useless, but I believe that most of it is and that I bear a burden which crushes me and does little to help any good end. It is impossible to say what a mess Ireland is and how everything enters into that mess. The Royal University is in the main, like the London University, an examining board. It does the work of examining well; but the work is not worth much. This is the first end I labour for and see little good in. Next my salary helps to support this college. The college is very moderately successful, rather a failure than a success, and there is less prospect of success now than before. Here too, unless things are to change, I labour for what is worth little. And in doing this almost fruitless work I use up all opportunity of doing any other.[22]

Never before Ireland had Hopkins passed such a judgement on his duties. He is not wretched because he is shackled as a poet but because of the futility of his life as a religious. He works for a college which is 'struggling for existence'[23] and unlikely to live long,[24] and so exhausting himself in his arid daily labours that he can find no energy for anything worth while. He has given himself over wholly in the Church's service only to find himself writing in 1889, 'I often think I am employed to do what is of little or no use'[25] – his anguish is scarcely to be wondered at.

The consequence for Hopkins' art is that in Ireland, in the years till his death from typhoid fever on 8 June 1889, his greatest poems turn away from beauty. The turning is involuntary, but it marks a breaking of the bounds which confined so much of his earlier work: the very fact of the involuntariness brings about a new development in him. The world is in its inner characteristics tempest-blown, barren, mountainous, frightful; it is bruised and blind. Its sounds are cries and hammer-blows, its tastes gall and bitterness.

It was a world which had always threatened him. For a man of fine sensibility, misery was a permanent possibility in the life which Hopkins led. His work as a Jesuit priest sent him into the great cities of the north – Liverpool, Glasgow, Preston – and this grimy urban living always depressed him. Liverpool was 'this horrible place'[26] and Glasgow a 'wretched place...like all our great towns'.[27] In this work, however, he was being used to some Catholic purpose and perpetually there was the likelihood of relief. His Society was, it seemed to him, continually on the move. 'Ours can never be an abiding city,' he wrote to his mother, '...and it is our pride to be ready for instant despatch.'[28] To Bridges he wrote: 'permanence with us is ginger-bread permanence; cobweb, soapsud, and frost-feather permanence',[29] and in 1880, twelve years after he joined the Jesuits, he evidently looked forward to change; he wrote from Liverpool, 'I do not think I can be long here; I have been long nowhere yet. I am brought face to face with the deepest poverty and misery in my district.'[30] Then he found himself established in Ireland, a kind of exile. Dublin too is 'a joyless place',[31] but now, with no promise of return, the effect of the joylessness is cumulative. 'Change is the only relief, and that I can seldom get.'[32] He loves country life and dislikes any town, 'especially for its bad and smokefoul air'.[33] His dream is 'a farm in the Western counties, glowworms, new milk...but in fact I live in Dublin'.[34] The constant changing of appointments is at an end in one that we can recognise from our position as being a well-intentioned attempt to make good use of his talents, but which in the event was only a match on paper: a scholar for a job needing scholarship. The consequence is not security but frequent strain.

In the past his poetry and his happiness had been tied together, the one bidden by the other. In Glasgow 'the vein urged by any country sight or feeling of freedom or leisure (you cannot tell what a slavery of mind or heart it is to live my life in a great town) soon dried',[35] and the pattern outlined here had shown before. Liverpool was 'of all places the most museless',[36] and 'My muse turned utterly sullen in the Sheffield smoke-ridden air.'[37]

Yet in Ireland this is reversed. He is writing poems not about delight so much as about the frequent misery of his life. Unhappiness, instead of completely stifling his poetry, is so acute that his poems become not a wish but a need, some of them 'like inspirations unbidden and against my will'.[38] He says, 'I want the one rapture of an inspiration'; yet there he is, writing poetry about the lack of this 'fine delight' ('To R. B.'). He appeals, 'Mine, O thou lord of life, send my roots rain'; yet the appeal comes in one of the most eloquent poems he ever wrote ('Thou art indeed just, Lord'), and we are confronted with the paradox that he is creating great poetry about his need to create: the misery he feels to be ending his art is, in fact, increasing its stature.

Many of Hopkins' Irish poems were a reaction to circumstances plainly uncongenial; they derive, then, from something external to the man, and are not the unprompted generations of something entirely private to him; they are not idiosyncratic. It is necessary to insist on this because, despite the plain truth of the situation given so often in his letters, and outlined above, the contrary is so often presumed to be the case. However, to insist on the commonsense view that it was his experience in Ireland which produced these poems is hardly to put them within reach of the glib inadequacies of common sense (the sort of common sense which summarises Hopkins' situation with the words, 'he died at a comparatively early age, having been more learned than practical'[39]): others, if similarly placed, might have been unhappy also, but the acuteness of both feeling and intelligence in the poems is Hopkins' own. It is for such acuteness in such extremity, for their going right to the edge of order, that they are valuable.

Hopkins had given his allegiance to the Society of Jesus and in consequence had been sent away from his own country, to which he felt such strong devotion, to a life of unproductive labour. His feelings about, and his judgement on, his job were at odds with his vow of obedience. Was it really God's will? On the one hand a sense of a life wasted, in every way unproductive; on the other, a vow to be kept: the opposition between the two provides the dynamic for much of his poetry in Ireland. *To* what, *for* what, was he responsible?

'Spelt from Sibyl's Leaves' begins by appearing to suggest that he is helpless. Having no control, he bears no blame either. The poem is full of tractional and torsional stresses (felt in the verse and evident in its 'strains–wound–hung–overbend–unbound–wind–spools' language), as though the tightening and slackening movements of the rack on which Hopkins finds himself at its close were being worked already. The unbinding of earth's being in the octave – a sort of laxness and Pandora's-box release of mobs – prefigures the attempted unbinding of the poet's own being which is referred to in the sestet as a forcible unravelling of the skeins which go to his own making. Again, the beaten pulp of 'self ín self steepèd and páshed', where things lose their distinctness and identity, anticipates in its anarchy the telling 'each off the other' of the sestet's colliding attempts to find an ordered single core of being.

At the outset no attempt seems possible. As 'stupendous' as the unnamed wrestler of the second quatrain in 'Carrion Comfort' is strong, evening closes down on life in terms so absolute that nothing can be done. As the first long, slow words show, there is more here than the temporary encroachment of dark on day: all realities are lost in the night which at once images them and cancels them as the final container, the ultimate surround, 'tíme's vást, ᐟ womb-of-all, home-of-all, hearse-of-all'. The poet who had exclaimed, 'Glory be to God for dappled things', now pronounces of earth, 'her dapple is at an end', and this, for Hopkins, is a new finality; not the finality of 'The Wreck of the Deutschland' which is ineluctable death, but one of a disorder which has to be lived through. There is, it seems, no control in this 'earthless' evening. Patterns have been broken by the darkness and, like animals or insects, have gone wild, as indistinguishable as the word 'throughther' which mimics the confusion. This is reality, and the order imposed by relatedness, the order of memory, is lost in – as it were – an old man's mumble, 'disremembering' showing the distractedness it describes. But order is recovered from the hostile night where the boughs of trees, hard-edged against the sky, stand in black silhouette, their leaves like beaks or the scales of dragons' backs – not less hostile, but a beginning-point for reason

to work. It is from these leaves, which are in word play the leaves or
pages of the Sibyl's books, that a prophecy for us is to be spelt out.
In the colourless contrast between the utterly black leaves and the
uniform bleakness of that part of the sky which they 'damask' lies
the only possibility of making sense of things – and it comes from a
pattern.

In writing the poem, there (at 'Our tale'), for two years, Hopkins
stopped.[40] He had read a prophecy already earlier in the poem: how
could he read another without being false to 'Óur évening is over us;
óur night ' whélms, whélms, ánd will end us'? For the first insists
that against the incomprehensible blankness of night there is nothing
to be done, and, though the prophecy is read for the future (it '*will*
end us'), in the poem it is being fulfilled already. Our evening is
'over us' in supremacy, upturned ('whelms') upon us: we await the
same fate as the rest of the earth. But the mood of the poem is one of
stiffening resistance, a resistance well given in a comment of Michael
Black's on the sestet: 'The four "buts" have an extraordinary effect:
of expostulation, of digging in the heels, but being dragged there all
the same.'[41] The terms in which Hopkins finally continued it share
in the ambiguity which is present in 'Carrion Comfort' also, an
ambiguity between action and passivity, subjection and defiance.
The night, which till the sestet has been characterised only by its
'earlstars' and its otherwise uninterrupted 'attuneable' harmonious
darkness, is moral, and everything must go into its terms, everything
must be destroyed in an unravelling that knows only the categories
right and wrong. The onset of nightfall, when the intricate web of
life is unwoven and, regardless of its colouring, seen only in terms of
black and white, is a correlative for the moral agony of self-judge-
ment, for the afflictions of a conscience which operates its own day of
reckoning, denying any considerations but 'black, white; ' right,
wrong' – the heavy tramping shows the peremptoriness and lack of
subtlety in the categories, but it is out of step, the terms not match-
ing. Then life becomes only the ricochetting conflict between what
is right and what is not, or a pulling apart of oneself on 'a rack'. The
onset of night is an augury of the division of the sheep and the goats
on the Day of Judgement, penned in two folds, but *that* judgement
is simple in its singleness; the poet is involved in something much

more complex. The clash of right and wrong is happening inside his own mind, is happening and is unresolved even as the poem ends.

The beginning of the poem does not promise such a finish; at the outset matters seem to be decided, and it is only in the sestet that an element of personal resolution is introduced, lingering uncertainly in the word 'Let'. Is this an instruction, or a conditional? Does it point at what must be, or at what may be? The first seems to be true in each case, but 'mind' and 'ware' not only tell us to take note but also introduce possibilities for evasion. The 'rack' we should obviously wish to avoid: 'Let' has submerged within it the sense 'if we let', and the consequence is that the poet not only has a measure of control over his predicament, he has to that extent a measure of responsibility for it also. The colour and variety and distinctness of all that we call beautiful may be undone and made general in the moral: there is the merest suggestion in this poem that the poet himself is responsible for winding off the skeins.

In 'Carrion Comfort' the question of control is central; the skeins which in 'Spelt from Sibyl's Leaves' go to make the world's patterned variety are here strands which, like those in a laid rope, are twisted together to make a man's being and moral strength: it is Hopkins who must keep them joined. He does so by an effort of will, and it is with this that the poem opens, Hopkins struggling to preserve a residual humanity by not giving way to despair. His is the plight of the hungry man tempted to feed on putrid flesh (Despair, by that device being given a separate objective existence, and in that way being managed as something external to the poet's core of identity). Against this desperate, horrible, and poisonous attraction Hopkins can set only his own determination: he will

> Not untwist – slack they may be – these last strands of man
> In me ór, most weary, cry *I can no more*. I can;

In the final, emphatic 'I can' lies the poem's moral strength, but set against this resolution is the awful difficulty of any practical action. The course is a vague 'Can something'. The proffered answers to the implicit question (can what?) are all attitudes of mind – 'hope', 'wish', or the merely passive 'not choose not to be'. How slender and precarious in that last course is the determination shown, and how paradoxical, for it shows only by *not* determining – this is the very limit of control, and it is most admirable in Hopkins that he could achieve it, that having 'failed so often'[42] he did persist, for to despair would be to dislocate success as a potential within oneself, would be to accept failure as a real expression of one's humanity. The persistent will to resist shown in this poem is the life-force, the will fully to be.

In the second quatrain the giant adversary of 'The Wreck of the Deutschland' is present as an unrecognised wrestler whose blows are a metaphor for the sufferings Hopkins endures in Ireland, in part at least the same conscience-rackings with which 'Spelt from Sibyl's Leaves' closes. Of the wrestler's superiority there is no doubt. The pressure he applies is gentle. He 'rocks' a foot and 'lays' a limb, yet still the poet's bones are bruised. The adversary is puzzling. His eyes 'scan' and 'devour' in eager examination, but he himself is inscrutable, terrifying. The poet, 'frantic to avoid thee and flee', can find no explanation for his suffering, though 'fan' in its primary technical sense begins to hint at one.

Not until the sestet does the iterated 'why?' prompt some kind of answer. This beating is a winnowing, 'That my chaff might fly; my grain lie, sheer and clear' – Hopkins' misery in Ireland is a test of his faith – but, just as he is about to confirm the suggested explanation, to make his mind up about its significance, he falters:

> Nay in all that toil, that coil, since (seems) I kissed the rod,
> Hand rather, my heart lo! lapped strength, stole joy, would laugh, chéer.

'Nay in all that toil' signals the arrival of some affirmative statement, but this positiveness evaporates in 'lapped', 'stole', and 'would' (i.e. 'wanted to'), and his confidence breaks on the word 'seems'. Has he in fact submitted? Was it obedience – the obedience which is given despite all personal inclination – or was it affection, and thus agreeable? The only things he can be sure of are ambiguous: that he has relished such strength as he could find, stolen joy, desired laughter. Which was wrong? – wanting joy so badly, or getting so little? The correctness of even this scanty pleasure is immediately put in question. The struggle breaks out again,

> Cheer whom though? The hero whose heaven-handling flung me,
>   fóot tród
> Me? or me that fought him? O which one? is it each one?

This is a nightmare world in that the poet cannot be sure of what is happening, or even of the significance of events which he does recognise. Even in the last lines of the poem, which try to end the experience by seeing it as something past, he fails. The 'night' becomes a 'year' of darkness, and Hopkins' attempt to define – and thus limit - the experience founders in the process of definition as new knowledge breaks over him. The adversary's identity is only now realised, he was '(my God!) my God!' and the juxtaposition of oath and allegiance, phonetically identical, semantically at polar extremes, points up the struggle which has been waged obscurely throughout the whole poem. This is the final irony, that the contest, apparently resolved, goes on even in the moment of resolution. In the terms of the powerful Biblical analogue for the last two-thirds of the poem,[43] Hopkins is Jacob, struggling as much with the limits of understanding as with those of faith.

It is the poem itself which is the control, the victory, the 'not untwisting' – to have been through *that* and written *this* – yet autobiography is not art, though in Hopkins' case, in these years, the two seem to work constantly to assimilate each other. For the reader, the abstracts of will and mind with which the poet is concerned have their existence only in the concrete particulars of dead flesh, unravelled strands, bruised bones, tempest winds, grain; it is the situation into which we are thus taken, the shaped context, which finally holds the poem's meaning. We are interested in Hopkins' mental anguish for the same reason that we are interested in Burns' love 'like a red, red rose' – because he presented it thus; but Burns' love is not of the order of experience which threatens the very means by which we come to know of it: some of Hopkins' Irish sonnets function within the situations they present, and as a means of delimiting; they determine his world. Thus it is difficult not to see these sonnets as a kind of therapy, for what is set down on paper is thereby fixed in the public medium of words and, to that extent, under control. Inasmuch as the poet thus needs language the process is involuntary; and some such pattern of dependence I take to underlie Hopkins' (perhaps defensive) comment to Bridges that four sonnets he wrote in Ireland came against his will.[44]

Of no poem are these remarks more true than of 'No worst, there is none', which is written with an imaginative intensity outside the range of Hopkins' contemporaries. It takes the afflictions of 'Spelt from Sibyl's Leaves' and 'Carrion Comfort' to a new pitch: the 'wretch' is fighting for that basic security without which there is no sanity.

The poem has been attacked in terms which seem to me to constitute a central challenge to what it is, and which bear on the question just raised of the relation between art and autobiography. Yvor Winters says,

he cannot move us by telling us why he himself is moved, he must try to move us by belabouring his emotion. He says, in effect: 'Share my fearful emotion, for the human mind is subject to fearful emotions.' But why should we wish to share an emotion so ill sponsored? Nothing could be more rash. We cannot avoid sharing a part of it, for Hopkins has both skill and genius; but we cannot avoid being confused by the experience[45]

Now we do not always trust those who answer us with reasons, and I think it would make little difference if one were to supply a single cause 'why he himself is moved'; I suspect Yvor Winters' unease would remain. The poem is not about causes, for it is an attempt to comprehend something which is of its nature unlocalised, and to supply a cause would be to give a location and render the attempt unnecessary. These points may become clearer in contrast with a poem by Oscar Wilde called 'Requiescat' (given in full), which I choose not as a success but precisely because emotion is so obviously running loose in it:

> Tread lightly, she is near
>   Under the snow,
> Speak gently, she can hear
>   The daisies grow.
>
> All her bright golden hair
>   Tarnished with rust,
> She that was young and fair
>   Fallen to dust.
>
> Lily-like, white as snow,
>   She hardly knew
> She was a woman, so
>   Sweetly she grew.
>
> Coffin-board, heavy stone
>   Lie on her breast,
> I vex my heart alone
>   She is at rest.

> Peace, Peace, she cannot hear
> Lyre or sonnet,
> All my life's buried here
> Heap earth upon it.

These five stanzas are Wilde's attempt to accept into his life the fact of a death. They begin by being sentimental and stylised. He says 'she can hear the daisies grow' when she obviously cannot; she is 'Lily-like, white as snow' – traditionally pure, that is; and the feelings offered are disconcertingly external. The last stanza frees itself from this by lurching in the other direction. It is in flat contradiction to the opening one which is seen as merely wishful now; 'she cannot hear'. Wilde is far from achieving the sort of calm which the opening so spuriously offered; he is overcome:

> All my life's buried here
> Heap earth upon it.

To deal with the fact of final separation, with death and burial, is to deal also with the emotion which these things engender (I am not, of course, suggesting that the emotion is cancelled or dispensed with, but that these are the terms in which it is to be comprehended).

Hopkins has no such recourse. It is in the nature of his misery that it is regenerative: 'More pangs will, schooled at forepangs, wilder wring'. It is not, then, a momentary or occasional thing, but something which is persistent and undefined, for the opening words of the poem show that the awesome thing about this experience is that it is without the sort of defining limit that Yvor Winters would like to see there, the limit imposed in Wilde's poem by the girl's death. Hopkins has said, not that there is nothing 'worse' than this, but that there is 'No worst'; the prediction is for suffering which, at this stage in the poem, has no foreseeable limit.

It is a prediction unfulfilled in the poem, for the twelve lines which follow are a reaction against it. Hopkins' appeals to the Comforter (the Paraclete)[46] and to the protecting Mary are cries which the poem itself takes up in its struggle to get far enough away from the experience of the first lines to be able to understand what is happening ('comfort' will be provided, like a physical shelter under which we crawl, and which was implicitly sought by the 'sheathe-and shelterless' one of 'Spelt from Sibyl's Leaves'):

> My cries heave, herds-long; huddle in a main, a chief-
> woe, world-sorrow; on an age-old anvil wince and sing –
> Then lull, then leave off. Fury had shrieked 'No ling-
> ering! Let me be fell: force I must be brief'.

'Heave' suggests the involuntary motions of physical sickness; from such involuntariness, as from a sobbing release, comes the first sign of relief. As cattle huddle together before a storm for comfort, so Hopkins finds consolation as his sufferings are joined with those of the human race, a 'world-sorrow'. The blows of 'Carrion Comfort' are delivered here across an anvil (Professor MacKenzie suggests that the idea is drawn from Hephaestus' riveting the fetters of Prometheus, pinned to a rock in punishment)[47] but it is an age-old one: there is reassurance in that this has happened before, there is pain and a cry and then the suffering will 'lull' and 'leave off'. The shrieking of Fury (a conflation of the Greek goddesses of vengeance) confirms the promise of that comfort for which the poet had cried out: the misery may be 'fell', cruel, and oppressive, but its very ferocity will mean that only for a little while can it be endured.

Only now in the sestet does it become clear that what we have been presented with is a mind at the furthermost reaches of sanity (the experience has been enacted for us like a miniature drama, the shrieked word 'lingering' dragged out across a line-ending and thus displaying its meaning). But to have seen that and said that any earlier would have been to introduce that element of control which was all the while being sought. Only now do we see what we have drawn back from; no man has been there *and* understood:

> O the mind, mind has mountains; cliffs of fall
> Frightful, sheer, no-man-fathomed.

Perhaps, Hopkins having drawn back to a distance where we can understand and feel secure, the suggestion that this is what was going on seems unconvincing or histrionic, so he insists on the precariousness of the position: 'Hold them cheap / May who ne'er hung there.' Between normality and *that* there is but little transaction; we cannot manage so for long.

The poem begins with echoes of Edgar's

> And worse I may be yet; the worst is not
> So long as we can say 'This is the worst'.[48]

It takes us, as if into Lear's hovel, 'under a comfort serves in a whirlwind', and it ends with Macbeth's sleep, 'The death of each day's life' (– and 'balm of hurt minds').[49] We cannot last long in such desperate circumstances, but in that very fact, in Fury's brevity, lies the comfort the wretch grovels for, the unassailable universality of 'all/Life death does end and each day dies with sleep'. The relief promised is future and permanent, temporary and soon.

Hopkins had written a poem about the approach of madness. The anxiety may well have been wholly mistaken, but it is one recurrent in his letters for that year (1885), and what matters more than any clinical estimate in this context is the fact that he felt the risk. He was as hard-pressed as that.[50] He wrote to Baillie,

The melancholy I have all my life been subject to has become of late years not indeed more intense in its fits but rather more distributed, constant, and crippling...when I am at the worst, though my judgment is never affected, my state is much like madness.[51]

The same fear was repeated in letters to Bridges: 'I think that my fits of sadness, though they do not affect my judgment, resemble madness';[52] 'soon I am afraid I shall be ground down to a state like last spring's and summer's, when my spirits were so crushed that madness seemed to be making approaches'.[53] Indeed, Hopkins' judgement was not affected, if it be a sign of unimpaired judgement to give careful and consistent assessment of a situation. The 'wretch' of 'No worst, there is none', like the 'wretch' of 'Carrion Comfort', struggles for that basic stability on which such judgement initially depends. When that stability is achieved in Hopkins' case, the resulting assessment of how things stand does not alter. Although different poems present differing attitudes to the situation, Hopkins' analysis is constant in its identification of the chief causes of his misery: that his work is laborious and of little value, that it so exhausts him that he can do nothing apart from it that is creative and worth while, that his life is thus wasted, that Ireland is foreign to him and that the Catholic Church there emphasises this by its involvement against the British government in the movement for home rule, that he himself must be to blame for being so impotent in all this. It is thus mistaken to point to the moments of happiness which Hopkins had in Ireland and to propose some pattern of desolation, struggle, and – finally –

victory (Ignatian or otherwise) in his life there. He kept his sanity and he did not despair; apart from this there were no victories to be sought or won, and he returned time and again to the same themes.

The retreat-notes he kept just a few months before his death are in a manner a synthesis of those themes. They show how little matters had changed in the four years since 1885.

I am now 44. I do not waver in my allegiance, I never have since my conversion to the Church. The question is how I advance the side I serve on. This may be inwardly or outwardly. Outwardly I often think I am employed to do what is of little or no use. Something else which I can conceive myself doing might indeed be more useful, but still it is an advantage for there to be a course of higher studies for Catholics in Ireland and that that should be partly in Jesuit hands; and my work and my salary keep that up. Meanwhile the Catholic Church in Ireland and the Irish Province in it and our College in that are greatly given over to a partly unlawful cause, promoted by partly unlawful means, and against my will my pains, laborious and distasteful, like prisoners made to serve the enemies' gunners, go to help on this cause. I do not feel then that outwardly I do much good, much that I care to do or can much wish to prosper; and this is a mournful life to lead. In thought I can of course divide the good from the evil and live for the one, not the other: this justifies me but it does not alter the facts. Yet it seems to me that I could lead this life well enough if I had bodily energy and cheerful spirits. However these God will not give me. The other part, the more important, remains, my inward service.

I was continuing this train of thought this evening when I began to enter on that course of loathing and helplessness which I have so often felt before, which made me fear madness and led me to give up the practice of meditation except, as now, in retreat and here it is again. I could therefore do no more than repeat *Justus es, Domine, et rectum judicium tuum* and the like, and then being tired I nodded and woke with a start. What is my wretched life? Five wasted years almost have passed in Ireland. I am ashamed of the little I have done, of my waste of time, although my helplessness and weakness is such that I could scarcely do otherwise. And yet the Wise Man warns us against excusing ourselves in that fashion. I cannot then be excused; but what is life without aim, without spur, without help? All my undertakings miscarry: I am like a straining eunuch. I wish then for death: yet if I died now I should die imperfect, no master of myself, and that is the worst failure of all. O my God, look down on me

Jan. 2 – This morning I made the meditation on the Three Sins, with nothing to enter but loathing of my life and a barren submission to God's will. The body cannot rest when it is in pain nor the mind be at peace as long as something bitter distills in it and it aches. This may be at any time and is at many: how then can it be pretended there is for those who feel this anything worth calling happiness in this world? There is a happiness, hope, the anticipation of happiness hereafter: it is better than happiness, but it is not happiness now. It is as if one were dazzled by a spark or star in the dark, seeing it but not seeing by it: we want a light shed on our way and a happiness spread over our life[54]

Not only the themes of the poems but some of their language shows here, and, more importantly, we have the sort of alternation of attitude which is evident in them also. In the first paragraph there is a sense of scrupulous care as in the compilation of a record. His consciousness of the futility of his work is qualified by 'I often think', the Irish cause is 'partly unlawful', promoted by 'partly unlawful means'. His efforts are 'laborious and distasteful' – the adjectives are restrained – and his life 'mournful'. In the second paragraph restraint has broken and the language is impassioned. His time is 'wasted', his life 'wretched'; he is 'ashamed', caught up in 'loathing and helplessness', 'a straining eunuch'. In the last paragraph his feelings have abated; he is the just man unjustly denied: 'how can it be pretended', not 'how can I pretend'. However, the points of grievance remain; the submission to God is 'barren'.

There are poems written in Ireland which focus specifically on that barrenness (and others where it is an important consideration), but in sequence they come towards the close of his life and it is another group, almost certainly written in 1885, which provides the essential connection between the mental uncertainties of the poems so far discussed in this chapter and the later insistent demand to be allowed, as a central right and responsibility, to create. It is to this group that I turn now.

The four sonnets which form this group, 'To seem the stranger', 'I wake and feel', 'Patience, hard thing!' and 'My own heart let me more have pity on', are attempts, not at understanding, but at resignation. These poems, written on two sides of a sheet of paper (which may, of course, result from no more than the convenience of a fair copy), are parts of a common process: the first two establish a fixity ('my lot', 'God's decree', 'the curse') with which the second two seek ways of coming to terms (patience *can* come, Hopkins must 'leave comfort root-room').

In 'To seem the stranger' all Hopkins' grievances turn on a single axis: that he is among strangers, an exile:

> To seem the stranger lies my lot, my life
> Among strangers. Father and mother dear,
> Brothers and sisters are in Christ not near
> And he my peace/my parting, sword and strife.

England, whose honour O all my heart woos, wife
To my creating thought, would neither hear
Me, were I pleading, plead nor do I: I wear-
y of idle a being but by where wars are rife.

I am in Ireland now; now I am at a third
Remove. Not but in all removes I can
Kind love both give and get. Only what word

Wisest my heart breeds dark heaven's baffling ban
Bars or hell's spell thwarts. This to hoard unheard,
Heard unheeded, leaves me a lonely began.

'I am in Ireland now' – how simple, direct, and doom-laden in the charge it derives from the previous and contrasting praise of England; and upon this exile he puts the blame for his failure to create: he is never separated from affection, but he is barred and thwarted. If he were in England he might 'breed', for England commands his allegiance (whereas Ireland implicitly does not); but the move to Ireland is seen by Hopkins as but a further, more extreme example ('a third/Remove', and hence a step further still from the things that count) of a truth which has determined his life. The stroke which makes 'peace' and 'parting' interchangeable is Hopkins' means of showing, even when surrounded by people, the essential isolation of the self whose idealism makes such aloneness an inevitable consequence; this poem is the lament of a man permanently bereft of a community he can call his own, reasoning outward from present circumstances – as wretchedness does – to make them a universal rule, a revelation of fundamental truth, rather than finite and contingent. Even England, he feels, would effectively disregard him if he tried to exercise any influence on the way her affairs are conducted, and he is tired of standing by ineffectually 'where wars are rife'. (In this and subsequent years Hopkins was to write that Gladstone, the 'Grand Old Mischief-maker',[55] 'a traitor to government in a great way and a danger on an imperial scale,'[56] 'negotiates his surrenders of the empire' while the race 'gapes on'.[57]) Even his family are remote from him, in religious terms, and the Biblical warning about Christ bringing the sword of separation[58] has come true. Indeed, the role of stranger has been cast for him as his destiny, yet (implicit in 'To *seem*') it is circumstance which traps him, not he who is responsible. He can petition heaven about his failure to create (in which case his prayers are 'Heard unheeded'), but there is no one with whom he can share his frustration, he must 'hoard' it 'unheard'.

For the 'lonely began' of 'To seem the stranger' there is no immediate way out. He is caught by either 'heaven's...ban' or the thwarting magic of hell – it may be one or the other, or it may be both; Hopkins is not sure. In 'I wake and feel' the situation is worse, the 'spell' has become a 'curse', and that of a kind which – the obvious rational explanation for the line apart – seems to involve a diabolic sorcery:

> I am gall, I am heartburn. God's most deep decree
> Bitter would have me taste: my taste was me;
> Bones built in me, flesh filled, blood brimmed the curse.

The making of man becomes in this last line a grotesque reduction that uses the physical constituents of his body as the ingredients in some hideous witches' recipe, an anti-life. It is as if the singleness of 'what I do is me' ('As kingfishers catch fire'), robbed of its initiative, had become 'I am my experience', or the consciousness, taken up wholly with the taste of the 'flesh-burst' sloe ('The Wreck of the Deutschland', stanza 8), had found it sour. It is paradoxical that this feeling of sourness which has its origin in sensitivity, in the openness to experience which produces the ecstasy of some of Hopkins' work, should here result in a closing off of change; for Hopkins here presents the idea expressed in his devotional writings that a self and a nature are joined by God in separate and seemingly arbitrary stages[59] – in Father Devlin's words, 'as if a man could be saddled with a nature fundamentally out of tune with his destiny'.[60] We have the same reasoning outward from present circumstances to things always presumed to be true that shows in 'To seem the stranger', but this poem is far more bitter and resentful. God decided even before the start that the poet should be the loathsome thing he is, Hopkins says, and his life was the inevitable fulfilment of the edict; his life was the activation of a curse. In this poem a disturbed night becomes by its blackness a symbol for a lifetime, but the poem goes further still:

> Selfyeast of spirit a dull dough sours. I see
> The lost are like this, and their scourge to be
> As I am mine, their sweating selves; but worse.

This is disappointed idealism that would rather take upon itself the blame than move the responsibility elsewhere, but, inasmuch as it makes a fixed thing the cause, it denies itself hope. The spirit's aspirations, proving too much for the laggard temperament (the 'dull dough'), sour it; and to be thus constantly involved with the persistent inner demand and a personal capacity or potential inadequate to meet it is, Hopkins says, like being damned.

Hopkins' sense of uniqueness, of self tasted 'at one tankard' only,[61] becomes in this poem self-loathing, and its oppressiveness is indicated from the very first line, where night presses upon him like a skin as something touched rather than seen. With the sort of poison working here 'To seem the stranger' has nothing in common, but 'I wake and feel' takes up the theme of loneliness with which the first poem is concerned when Hopkins writes of 'cries countless' – continuing and unheard appeals to God which are like unanswered letters sent to Robert Bridges, 'dearest him that lives alas! away'.[62] There is an interlinking also between the failure to create, which is a major theme in 'To seem the stranger', and the 'ruins' of 'Patience, hard thing!' In the second poem the wrecks are accepted as things to be lived with, for the poet chastens the impatience which initially has its way. The last line of the first quatrain, which recalls the vows of poverty, chastity, and obedience, points at the dilemma Hopkins faced in Ireland:

> Patience, hard thing! the hard thing but to pray,
> But bid for, Patience is! Patience who asks
> Wants war, wants wounds; weary his times, his tasks;
> To do without, take tosses, and obey.
>
> Rare patience roots in these, and, these away,
> Nowhere.

Patience is an elusive and paradoxical virtue, for whoever wants it is in part possessed of it already. The hard thing, says Hopkins, is to wish to be patient in the first place; the quality of patience is never required where there is excitement. No one engaged in active warfare ever needs it (the poet, we remember from 'To seem the stranger', is 'idle...where wars are rife'), but only those whose lives and whose jobs are dull. Patience is inextricable from monotony – which makes it appear an unattractive quality – but when patience grows, as it does once it takes hold, it makes failure endurable. It becomes not a severe and unpalatable discipline, but ease; patience is a waiting – all day.

> Natural heart's ivy, Patience masks
> Our ruins of wrecked past purpose. There she basks
> Purple eyes and seas of liquid leaves all day.

In these lines we can see the seemingly intuitive movement of Hopkins' thought, carrying in this case within the imagery the conscious tensions of the poem. He seems unaware of the image as such and does not, like Donne, exercise over it a mathematic and qualifying control. Instead of considering further the relation between the ivy and the 'wrecked past purpose' he allows the image to multiply, and out of the phrase comes 'seas of liquid leaves' and then the further 'We hear our hearts grate on themselves', which might be based on the idea of pebbles moved by waves. There is, however, another possibility for this last sentence, relating to the absence of conscious consideration – a Shakespearian absence, for, it is well known, Shakespeare, too, made brilliant intuitive use of the mixed metaphor. In 'Our ruins of wrecked past purpose' there are two potential lines of development, one which deals with ruins of a building, and another which deals with wrecks of ships. Ivy grows over the ruins attractively as something rooted and firm, consoling. However, the notion of shipwreck still competes even with the apparent domination of the solid and sure: 'seas of liquid leaves' keeps the element of involuntariness and pain and insecurity which reasserts itself in the 'grate' of the following line, the grating of the wreck upon the shore, a restatement, at any rate, of the condition for which patience was first invoked. It is obvious that covering ivy is irrelevant to wrecked ships, but there is another sign too that the initial victory of patience was not the final one: 'masks' and 'eyes' make it a matter of sight, of appearances, whereas we 'hear' beneath the surface the struggle still continue. The imagery of wreck and ruin is abandoned for the honeycombs of sweet kindness, filled by patience's slow secretion.

It is only its context which makes 'Patience, hard thing!' akin to the poems which precede it. In the juxtaposition one can see how it acts as a corrective to their dejection, but in seeking consolation

Hopkins was falling back on calmer moments experienced before he went to Ireland. He had written about patience seven years earlier, tying it to peace in the poem of that name, where 'Peace' is as elusive as patience is here. That sort of return may perhaps be evident also at the close of 'My own heart let me more have pity on'. Ireland also has its mountains, but it was in Wales where he studied amongst them that Hopkins was happiest. At the start of the poem his thoughts so tyrannise that he lives not a life but a 'tormented mind'; everything else is blotted out. He is so caught in its involutions (as, in 'I wake and feel', he was so preoccupied with the taste of his own bitterness) that he can share only *its* processes; comfort has no place inside it. Light alone cannot cure blindness; mere wetness, however widespread, is no substitute for a quantity of water to drink; frantic searching is equally doomed – the very activity of the questing hounds of thought is the cause of the problem, for as patience will grow unbidden so comfort will *happen*, it will not be a *willed* thing. The 'self-yeast' and the 'dull dough' of 'I wake and feel' have become here the tormenting mind – the aspirer – and the 'poor Jackself', the heart, living mundanely:

> Soul, self; come, poor Jackself, I do advise
> You, jaded, let be; call off thoughts awhile
> Elsewhere; leave comfort root-room; let joy size
>
> At God knows when to God knows what; whose smile
> 's not wrung, see you; unforeseen times rather – as skies
> Betweenpie mountains – lights a lovely mile.

Think of something other than what you must do; your thoughts are so monopolising all space that there is no room for comfort; comfort must come independently, unsought, unbidden – thus the quiet, authoritative voice of a consultant or a confessor. Joy must take its size according to circumstance, and will not be forced. The poem ends by expecting, sometime, the unexpected. The sudden dappling of sky between mountains gives the light previously denied to 'blind / Eyes', and the 'lovely mile' relieves the poem's claustrophobic searching.

Hopkins thus counsels himself to the patience which he has sought previously in 'Patience, hard thing!', and such counsel involves the shedding of that mode of thought which makes rule its essential characteristic. He must avoid scrupulous introspection and become more elastic, be kinder and less stringent with himself, and this we have seen he did, giving up the practice of meditation except in retreat. However, dejection often overtook him nonetheless and his sense of having failed to finish his projects or to produce poems enough was persistent.

Might he, then, have written more if he had lived his life differently? The question is hypothetical and, in that sense, seemingly spurious, but it confronts anyone who studies Hopkins' poems because, in a way that is certainly not spurious, it asks for a judgement on the effect of the life Hopkins actually led. It is a question easily construed in terms which raise once more the issue of a dichotomy between his poetry and his priesthood: did he not as a poet make a disastrous mistake in joining the Jesuits? Hopkins himself connected his miseries in Ireland with his failure to create (his was a 'winter world' denied inspiration; it was England which was 'wife/To my creating thought'): was he justified in doing so?

Although he wrote more readily in Wales when he was free of responsibility and at his most relaxed, and although, even before his posting in Ireland, he blamed circumstances for his failure to produce any quantity of work, it seems to me that we should pay more attention to those other occasions when he admitted that someone else in the same position might have done more. Sometimes such admissions have about them that sense of harassment which makes one sceptical of the judgement they contain, but we have in addition the body of Hopkins' work as evidence. Especially with regard to his years in Ireland, it is difficult to recall adequately that the life Hopkins led was chosen: the tangle of frustration and disappointment and drudgery in which he found himself was a consequence of his pursuit of excellence, of the very idealism which sought something better and would not be content with such a tangle. The two – the loftiness of the ideal and the difficulty of trying to realise it in the imperfections of life – are inextricable one from another, and out of them comes his greatest poetry: the life made the art.

Writing to his Oxford friend Baillie after he had been sorting out letters going back even to his schooldays and looking through old notebooks, he remarked that he still had 'beginnings of things, ever so many, which it seems to me might well have been done, ruins and wrecks'.[63] When one sets that beside a letter he had written to the same correspondent twenty-one years earlier, one might readily conclude that he had in between made a calamitous mistake:

I have written a lot of my *Pilate*. I am thinking of a *Judas*, but such a subject is beyond me at present. I have added several stanzas to *Floris in Italy* but it gets on very slowly. I have nearly finished an answer to Miss Rossetti's *Convent Threshold*...I have written three religious poems which however you would not at all enter into, they being of a very Catholic character. Also *The Lover's Stars* (a trifle in something like Coventry Patmore's style), and a thing which I hope you will like, a soliloquy of one of the spies left in the wilderness, and the beginning of a story to be called *Richard*, and some other fragments. So, though I finish nothing, I am not idle...I have now a more rational hope than before of doing something – in poetry and painting.[64]

Hopkins is buoyant as he excitedly tumbles out his latest schemes, but how easily that mood might change is evident here: 'but it gets on very slowly', 'the beginning of a story', 'fragments', 'though I finish nothing' – perhaps some of these pieces were lost in Hopkins' burning; the only poems we know he completed were the ones he mentions as being written when he sent the letter. The others, excepting *Judas*, exist as fragments.

Additionally, when Dr Leavis asks – given 'Hopkins' impressive gift' – why 'the paradoxical meagreness'?[65] one feels that, sadly, the meagreness is not paradoxical at all. Much of the impressiveness of the gift lies in its tautness, and, whereas it is the weakness of fluency to become lax, the risk inherent in tautness is that *nothing* will result, that every attempt will be so exacting that it will produce only pages of erasures. Hopkins' genius for compression is a further characteristic sign of the nature of his gift. Few, if any, have packed so much meaning into the sonnet, and the sonnet was the form he habitually chose as the vehicle best suited to his intenseness – intenseness of feeling and compression being in him inseparable. The impressiveness of the gift lies also in the exacting technical standards which Hopkins set and so often matched, and here again the sonnet form, particularly the more difficult Petrarchan one which he characteristically employed, is a challenging one to work with. Such standards are daunting, and there are signs that Hopkins found them so. It seems that in his case the extreme technical demand had to be met by an equivalent strength in the inspiration and this was not often forthcoming: the rack on which his creativity suffered was that of his own rigour; surviving that, it had a claim to distinction.

Especially when one sees the wonderful fluency of his letters, one has the sense that his verse had to endure some constriction, and it was essentially the same constriction which operated in his spiritual life: he took both so very seriously. However, that seriousness is not just the seriousness indispensable where matters of faith are concerned – that displayed, for example, in Herbert's 'Redemption' – it is a seriousness touched with anxiety, as if in some matters he was wanting in the relaxed confidence that would enable him to hold with certainty to some truth that was not contained within the strong frame of law: he did not trust himself at certain crucial places. One of these was that of his own creativeness. This shows in the early 'The Alchemist in the City'.

In that poem it is the speaker's unhappy lot to be denied reward. He makes no progress, he remains as he was, and thus he introduces Hopkins' worry about failing to create. The poem is, indeed, Hopkins' first major act of self-criticism. It begins the line which leads to 'Thou art indeed just, Lord' with its remonstrations against failure; to the feeling of inadequacy in 'To R. B.'; to the isolation of 'To seem the stranger'; to the 'ruins of wrecked past purpose' in 'Patience, hard thing!'; and to the self-loathing of 'I wake and feel'.

The Alchemist is symbolic of all who try for the magnificent and risk failing even in the ordinary. His recondite practice acts equally well as an image for artistic creation and as one for laborious scholarship, but it seems to me mistaken to argue that either of these is specifically in question. The poem is diminished if it is read as an allegory. It is not the nature of his endeavour but the Alchemist's temperament which is at the core of the poem (I give the first five stanzas):

> My window shows the travelling clouds,
> Leaves spent, new seasons, alter'd sky,
> The making and the melting crowds:
> The whole world passes; I stand by.

They do not waste their meted hours,
But men and masters plan and build:
I see the crowning of their towers,
And happy promises fulfill'd.

And I – perhaps if my intent
Could count on prediluvian age,
The labours I should then have spent
Might so attain their heritage,

But now before the pot can glow
With not to be discover'd gold,
At length the bellows shall not blow,
The furnace shall at last be cold.

Yet it is now too late to heal
The incapable and cumbrous shame
Which makes me when with men I deal
More powerless than the blind or lame.

'Waste', 'shame'; 'I am ashamed of the little I have done, of my waste of time':[66] nearly a quarter-century separates these utterances of Hopkins', but the agreement of youth with middle age is striking – the more striking because the Alchemist whose identity the youthful poet has adopted is a man who has had his life, or, at least, the best part of it. He has written off what future is left to him: 'it is now too late'. Looking at the 'alter'd sky' he has very powerfully the sense that, with him, things will stay as they have been and as they are. Others bring their plans to fruition (just as in 1889 Hopkins wrote in 'Thou art indeed just, Lord', 'birds build – but not I build') but he is incapable of achievement; and his self-confessed gaucheness here is offered as something other than the awkwardness of youth.[67] Although the poet uses a persona in this poem, there is no irony to suggest any emotional distance between himself and his spokesman; we are justified in seeing Hopkins as the Alchemist, and the poem is thus very illuminating. It shows a pessimism and a melancholy which are ominous in someone twenty years old, and it reveals that the cause of this melancholy is in the temperament of the writer (the process is circular: the Alchemist has condemned himself even before his work has actually failed beyond all hope; his work must therefore fail, and the condemnation be justified). The image of the cooling furnace anticipates both the short-lived 'blowpipe flame' of inspiration in 'To R. B.' (1889) and also a comment in a letter of 1888:

It is now years that I have had no inspiration of longer jet than makes a sonnet, except only in that fortnight in Wales: it is what, far more than direct want of time, I find most against poetry and production in the life I lead.[68]

'The Alchemist in the City' is the product of a creative mind, fearful about the failing of its own processes.

It shares, in this sense, a common theme with a striking fragment from later that year (1865), of which I give the first four lines:

> Trees by their yield
> Are known; but I –
> My sap is sealed,
> My root is dry.

Here, as in the last plea of 'Thou art indeed just, Lord' ('send my roots rain'), the pattern of natural growth is used to express both the direction of his whole being and the sense that that direction is being frustrated. He has done nothing; he has gained no merit. 'I see no grounded prospect', Hopkins was to write from Stonyhurst in 1883, 'of my ever doing much not only in poetry but in anything at all.'[69] The feeling was to be repeated three and a half years after that in Ireland: 'It is so doubtful, so very doubtful, that I shall be able to pursue any study except the needs of the day...I have tried and failed so often.'[70] The same mind which was, paradoxically, to be creating poems about the need to create even up to its death, was doing the same in Oxford. The inward-turning anxiety at the core of the malaise was lifelong.

In part the sense of artistic aridity which Hopkins expresses in Ireland is connected with his dissatisfaction with the role of ineffectual bystander and his increasingly strong belief that art is in the largest sense political. He told Patmore that fine works of art are 'an element of strength even to an empire',[71] and Bridges received from him this clarion call:

I say it deliberately and before God, I would have you and Canon Dixon and all true poets remember that fame, the being known, though in itself one of the most dangerous things to man, is nevertheless the true and appointed air, element, and setting of genius and its works. What are works of art for? to educate, to be standards. Education is meant for the many, standards are for public use...We must then try to be known...Besides, we are Englishmen. A great work by an Englishman is like a great battle won by England. It is an unfading bay tree. It will even be admired by and praised by and do good to those who hate England (as England is most perilously hated), who do not wish even to be benefited by her. It is then even a patriotic duty τῇ ποιήσει ἐνεργεῖν [to be active in producing poetry] and to secure the fame and permanence of the work.[72]

That this last was a duty Hopkins did not himself undertake is well known. The undated fragment 'The times are nightfall' (of which I give the octave) suggests the reason:

> The times are nightfall, look, their light grows less;
> The times are winter, watch, a world undone:
> They waste, they wither worse; they as they run
> Or bring more or more blazon man's distress.
> And I not help. Nor word now of success:
> All is from wreck, here, there, to rescue one –
> Work which to see scarce so much as begun
> Makes welcome death, does dear forgetfulness.

Initially there seems to be little to differentiate this poem's concerns from the cosmic movements of 'Spelt from Sibyl's Leaves', but 'the times' are here what they would be anywhere else, political and social. Potentially it is within the poet's power to do something about the situation; he stands apart from it as one aware at least of what is happening, but then he offers as a sign of his helplessness the wreck of his own work from which he so vainly tries to salvage anything worth while. The three extant lines which follow this extract have him doing what he does in the retreat-notes cited earlier, turning from his 'outward service' to the 'world within', for 'Your will is law in that small commonweal' – it so obviously is not in the social world.

The same alternation between inner and outer worlds is the central theme in Hopkins' poem about another bystander, 'St. Alphonsus Rodriguez'. The poem is, of course, more about Hopkins than about the doorkeeper saint ('the brand' is one that 'we' wield); and he does not say that 'They also serve who only stand and wait' but that they do much more than wait and that they have a right to be noticed. Hopkins' poem constitutes such notice in Alphonsus' case. There are 'wars within' and 'the heroic breast' may be 'steeled' in ways other than being encased in armour, though all this goes unremarked.

> Yet God (that hews mountain and continent,
> Earth, all, out; who with trickling increment,
> Veins violets and tall trees makes more and more)
> Could crowd career with conquest while there went
> Those years and years by of world without event
> That in Majorca Alfonso watched the door.

Nature's role in the poem is ambivalent. The patterning of violets, the growth of trees, the change of landmass – the physical manifestations of a living earth – apparently contrast with Alphonsus' life which is explicitly 'without event'; but the force of that 'could', preceded as it is by the vast productivity of the maker, is such as to leave one with the sense that, with conquest, the life of Alphonsus *was* crowded: that is his – and Hopkins' – claim on attention.

The wrecks of 'Patience, hard thing!' and 'The times are nightfall', the frustration of 'To seem the stranger', and the implicit claim for consideration in 'St. Alphonsus Rodriguez' are gathered in 'Thou art indeed just, Lord' into a formidable disputation against failure. This poem turns the energy of agony which is felt in 'No worst, there is none' and 'I wake and feel' and 'Carrion Comfort' into a petitioning urgency which will brook no denial. God is reasoned against as the causer of sterility:

> Wert thou my enemy, O thou my friend,
> How wouldst thou worse, I wonder, than thou dost
> Defeat, thwart me? Oh, the sots and thralls of lust
> Do in spare hours more thrive than I that spend,
>
> Sir, life upon thy cause. See, banks and brakes
> Now, leavèd how thick! lacèd they are again
> With fretty chervil, look, and fresh wind shakes
>
> Them; birds build – but not I build; no, but strain,
> Time's eunuch, and not breed one work that wakes.
> Mine, O thou lord of life, send my roots rain.

Like Jeremiah, whose words, in paraphrase, open the poem, the poet is the just man arguing the age-old grievance that the righteous suffer and sinners are rewarded in their stead. The poem's opposition of 'the sots and thralls of lust' and 'Time's eunuch' establishes the denial sexually as a particularly intimate and humiliating kind; the lascivious effortlessly flourish and that exacerbates his feeling of impotence, as if by a display of sexual luxury to the impoverished. This could so easily have been mawkish and self-pitying, but the poem argues out, as if in a suit to a judge, a powerful natural justice. It insists with compelling reasonableness on the irrationality of treating friends as if they were enemies and denying them that which all nature has. Our attention is not on the advocate who makes the plea but on the one addressed, constantly identified for us as 'thou', 'lord', 'sir', and upon the argument advanced, eloquently with its Shakespearian cadence ('Oh, the sots and thralls of lust /Do in spare hours more thrive than I that spend, /Sir, life upon thy cause). Life has been given over to the lord's service, but there is no suggestion in the poem that this sacrifice is to blame, for, in the absence of any other claim, that cause becomes by attraction the one that is being advanced; the lord when he is titled is 'thou lord of life'.

'There be eunuchs', says the passage in Matthew's gospel from which Hopkins' image is taken, 'which have made themselves eunuchs for the kingdom of heaven's sake.'[73] The idea of such self-sacrifice as this entails was one Hopkins repeated in a letter to Bridges,[74] though without explaining how he thought the sacrifice had come about and whether it was voluntary or forced or coincidental in his view. Neither in this poem nor in that letter, nor in the other two places[75] where he uses this image, is he content with that lot. The power of sexuality, though it may be stimulated or checked or sublimated, is not of itself in nature within the scope of human choice. It is an automatic circuit. As the movements of the natural world are unsolicited by man so is this; indeed, it may be said to be the force of nature operating within man, what he – as a trammel, or as a consolation – has in common with the brute beasts of the field. In view of this, 'To R. B.', like 'Thou art indeed just, Lord', has a deep human centrality. It too is about impotence, though it begins so powerfully that it works in flat contradiction to its reasoned case. Its octave is Hopkins' distinctive version of what Wordsworth had so differently characterised as 'emotion recollected in tranquillity' – in its concreteness and its energy, amounting almost to indelicacy, how huge a gulf it marks:

> The fine delight that fathers thought; the strong
> Spur, live and lancing like the blowpipe flame,
> Breathes once and, quenchèd faster than it came,
> Leaves yet the mind a mother of immortal song.

> Nine months she then, nay years, nine years she long
> Within her wears, bears, cares and combs the same:
> The widow of an insight lost she lives, with aim
> Now known and hand at work now never wrong.
>
> Sweet fire the sire of muse, my soul needs this;
> I want the one rapture of an inspiration.
> O then if in my lagging lines you miss
>
> The roll, the rise, the carol, the creation,
> My winter world, that scarcely breathes that bliss
> Now, yields you, with some sighs, our explanation.

Even more markedly than 'Thou art indeed just, Lord' the opening
is strikingly sexual, the surge of inspiration at one with the rush of
semen; but this vital energy is quickly lost, and the gestation which
follows is so protracted that it challenges for pre-eminence the
poem's chief lament, that the bliss of inspiration is rare now. Now
the world Hopkins lives in is a winter one, opposed implicitly and
characteristically to the fecundity of spring, but the poem has about
it a remarkable assurance which it shares with 'Thou art indeed just,
Lord'. Once the inspiration has come it provides its own self-justifying and directing impulse, 'aim/Now known', 'work now never
wrong'. To maintain in the face of this new certitude that there was
any decline in Hopkins' poetic powers would be to mistake entirely
the significance of these last laments, to trust too readily in the
Alchemist and not sufficiently in the quality of the poems in which
the laments were uttered. When one looks at the three sonnets which
he wrote in the last months of his life one is given good grounds for
believing that, had he lived, Hopkins would only have strengthened
his already considerable claim on our attention.

He was ill when he sent Bridges the sonnet dedicated to him. The
illness, which coincided with 'the most pressing time of University
work', brought him unexpected relief. It worsened, but he endured
it cheerfully. 'At many such a time', he wrote to his mother, 'I have
been in a sort of extremity of mind, now I am the placidest soul in
the world.'[76] He was forty-four. The last waning movement of the
poem to Bridges is given by the chance fact of Hopkins' early death
the significance of an elegant adieu.

NOTES

LIST OF SYMBOLS

Poems The Poems of Gerard Manley Hopkins, 4th edn, ed. W. H. Gardner and
N. H. MacKenzie, London, 1967

RB The Letters of Gerard Manley Hopkins to Robert Bridges, ed. C. C. Abbott,
London, 1955

C The Correspondence of Gerard Manley Hopkins and Richard Watson Dixon,
ed. C. C. Abbott, London, 1955

FL Further Letters of Gerard Manley Hopkins, 2nd edn, ed. C. C. Abbott,
London, 1956

J The Journals and Papers of Gerard Manley Hopkins, ed. Humphry House,
completed by Graham Storey, London, 1959

S The Sermons and Devotional Writings of Gerard Manley Hopkins, ed.
Christopher Devlin, London, 1959

CHAPTER ONE: ALL SURRENDERS

1. *J* p. 71, 6 November 1865.
2. See William Empson, *Seven Types of Ambiguity*, 3rd edn, 1956, repr.
Harmondsworth, 1961, p. 225 (of 'The Windhover'): 'there may be some
reference to this sacrifice in the *fire* of the Sonnet'.
3. See Joseph Hillis Miller, *The Disappearance of God: Five Nineteenth-Century
Writers*, Cambridge, Mass., 1963, p. 335: 'In the end Hopkins finds that
poetry is not trivial or neutral, but, like other positive ways of affirming
selfhood, a means to damnation.'
4. *J* p. 165, 7 May 1868.
5. *FL* p. 39, 7 July 1867.
6. *FL* p. 408, quoted by Newman in his reply of 14 May 1868.
7. *FL* p. 434, 15 October 1866, from his father to the Rev. H. P. Liddon.
8. I Corinthians 9:27.
9. *RB* p. 47, 21 August 1877.
10. Elizabeth W. Schneider, *The Dragon in the Gate: Studies in the Poetry of
Gerard Manley Hopkins*, Berkeley and Los Angeles, 1968, p. 5.
11. *Ibid.* p. 4.
12. See *J* p. 381, n63:1.

13. *RB* p. 25, 29 April 1869.
14. *C* p. 6, 13 June 1878.
15. *FL* p. 386, 6 May 1888.
16. *RB* p. 43, 8 August 1877.
17. *C* p. 14, 5 October 1878.
18. See V. de Sola Pinto, *Crisis in English Poetry, 1820–1940*, London, 1951, p. 72: 'Stevenson's Dr Jekyll and Mr Hyde can be taken as a symbol of this poet. Dr Jekyll was the model Victorian scholar, the favourite pupil of Jowett, the friend of Newman and the saintly Catholic priest; Mr Hyde was the savage and sensual artist ... and the "communist".' Hopkins himself used the 'symbol' (*RB* p. 238, 28 October 1886), but that does not justify these remarks.
19. In his preface (*J* p. xx) Graham Storey gives his reasons for not publishing these confession-notes; namely because of their private nature, and because they are repetitious.
20. MS described in *J* p. 530 as C.II, and kept at Campion Hall, Oxford, p. 95.
21. *Ibid.* p. 103. Other references to scrupulosity about poetry and about other matters are to be found on pp. 103, 107, and 110.
22. *C* p. 8, 13 June 1878.
23. *FL* p. 38, 7 July 1867, to E. W. Urquhart.
24. *J* p. 258, 6 September 1874.
25. N. H. MacKenzie, *Hopkins*, London, 1968, p. 13.
26. *FL* p. 231, 12 February 1868.
27. *RB* p. 24, 7 August 1868.
28. *C* p. 14, 5 October 1878.
29. See *J* pp. 537–9, where Humphry House discusses Hopkins' *J* entry 'Slaughter of the Innocents', and points to the way in which Hopkins clearly linked three dates (23 August 1867, 2 May 1868, and 11 May 1868), the first two of which relate to a decision in the making, the third to an act consequent upon it. He rejects W. H. Gardner's suggestion that the decision concerned was to remain celibate (on the ground that this interpretation disregards Hopkins' careful cross-referencing) and notes that the *J* words 'I resolved' occur also in a reference to the burning of the poems (letter to Dixon): the decision in both cases was 'formally considered'. The poems had been destroyed by 7 August 1868 (letter to Bridges), and there is no other *J* entry relating to their burning. 'The conclusion seems inescapable that the slaughtered innocents were his poems, the children of his creation.' This view gives further support to the idea of the burning as a symbolic act.
30. *RB* p. 24, 7 August 1868.
31. *FL* p. 54, 2 July 1868, to Fr Ignatius Ryder.
32. *RB* p. 270, 12 January 1888.
33. *RB* p. 41, 13 June 1877.
34. *RB* p. 150, 26 September 1882.
35. *C* p. 14, 5 October 1878.
36. *RB* p. 197, 21 August 1884.
37. *C* p. 88, 2 November 1881.
38. *FL* p. 385, 6 May 1888.
39. *C* p. 88, 2 November 1881.

40. *S* p. 215.
41. *RB* p. 56, 16 July, 1878: 'The Hurrahing Sonnet was the outcome of half an hour of extreme enthusiasm.'
42. 'To R. B.': the one rapture of an inspiration'.
43. *RB* p. 178, 27 March, 1883.
44. *S* p. 218 (Devlin's ellipsis).
45. *C* p. 6, 13 June 1878.
46. *C* p. 88, 2 November 1881.
47. *C* pp. 93–4, 1 December 1881.
48. *C* p. 93, 1 December 1881.
49. *FL* p. 214, 20 July 1864.
50. *FL* p. 38, 7 July 1867.
51. *RB* p. 24, 29 April 1868.
52. *RB* p. 97, 22 October 1879.
53. *FL* p. 139, 26 June 1876.
54. *C* pp. 30–1, 31 October 1879.
55. *C* p. 132, 30 June 1886.
56. *S* pp. 253–4.
57. See *C* pp. 46–7, 28 March and 6 April 1881.
58. *RB* p. 128, 1 May 1881.
59. *Ibid.*
60. *FL* pp. 352–3.
61. *RB* p. 291, 25 September 1888.
62. *RB* p. 231, 13 October 1886.
63. *RB* p. 123, 7 February 1881.
64. *C* p. 8, 13 June 1878.
65. *RB* p. 179, 11 May, 1883.
66. *RB* pp. 77–8, 8 April 1879.
67. *FL* p. 36, 16 January 1867.
68. *RB* p. 46, 21 August 1877.
69. *RB* p. 50, 21 May 1878.
70. *RB* p. 80, 22 April 1879.
71. *C* p. 8, 13 June 1878.

CHAPTER TWO: PATER, AND THE FALCON

1. Walter Pater, 'Coleridge's Writings', *Westminster Review*, January, 1866; repr. in *English Critical Essays (Nineteenth Century)*, ed. Edmund D. Jones, London, 1950, pp. 421–57 (p. 427).
2. *Poems*, p. 139.
3. *Poems*, p. 164.
4. *Poems*, p. 130.
5. (W. H. Gardner, *Gerard Manley Hopkins 1844–1889: A Study of Poetic Idiosyncrasy in relation to Poetic Tradition*, 2 vols., London, 1958, vol. I, pp. 164–5.
6. *J* p. 66.
7. *J* p. 72.
8. *J* p. 137, 20 May 1866.

9. *J* p. 152, 6 July 1867.
10. *J* p. 153, 27 August 1867.
11. *J* p. 189, 21 October 1868.
12. *J* p. 192, September 1869.
13. *J* p. 222, 8 August 1872.
14. *J* p. 254, 17 August 1874.
15. *J* p. 17.
16. *J* p. 171, 10 July 1868.
17. *J* p. 209, 9 and 11 May 1871.
18. *J* p. 205, March 1871.
19. David A. Downes, *Gerard Manley Hopkins: A Study of His Ignatian Spirit*, New York, 1959, p. 166.
20. *Ibid.* pp. 54, 10.
21. *The Spiritual Exercises of Saint Ignatius Loyola*, trans. W. H. Longridge, London, 1919, p. 53.
22. E.g. 'to see with the eyes of the imagination the length, breadth, and depth of hell', *ibid.* pp. 66ff.
23. 'The colloquy is made, properly speaking, as a friend speaks to a friend, or a servant to his master, asking at one time for some grace, at another accusing oneself of some evil committed, at another making known one's affairs, and seeking counsel concerning them', *ibid.* p. 58.
24. Downes, *op. cit.* p. 74.
25. *Ibid.* pp. 74–5.
26. *Spiritual Exercises*, p. 26, 'Principle and Foundation'.
27. *Ibid.* p. 157.
28. *C* p. 75, 12 October 1881.
29. *RB* p. 172, 28 January 1883.
30. *FL* pp. 313–14, 28 September 1883, to Patmore.
31. *FL* p. 204, 6 September 1863, to Baillie.
32. *FL* p. 380, 20 October 1887, to Patmore.
33. *C* p. 73, 12 October 1881.
34. *FL* p. 257, 24 April 1885, to Baillie.
35. *FL* p. 38, 7 July 1867; p. 40, 15 August 1867 (to E. W. Urquhart).
36. *J* p. 167, 17 June 1868.
37. *RB* p. 48, 2 April 1878.
38. *FL* p. 246, to Baillie.
39. *J* p. 138, 31 May 1866.
40. *RB* p. 60, 19 January 1879.
41. *RB* p. 62, 29 January 1879.
42. I refer also to his essay 'The School of Giorgione', not published until October 1877 (in *The Fortnightly Review*, o.s. XXVIII, n.s. XXII, pp. 526–38) and subsequently included in *The Renaissance*, 3rd edn, London, 1888, pp. 135–61.
43. Walter Pater, *The Renaissance: Studies in Art and Poetry*, with an introduction by Kenneth Clark, London, 1961, pp. 220–1.
44. Pater, 'Coleridge's Writings', p. 422.
45. *Ibid.* p. 422.
46. *Ibid.* p. 422.

47. *Ibid.* p. 456.
48. Pater, *Renaissance*, p. 222.
49. Pater, 'Coleridge's Writings', p. 423.
50. *Ibid.* pp. 423–4.
51. *Ibid.* p. 457.
52. *J* p. 120, 'The Probable Future of Metaphysics' (1867).
53. *J* p. 120.
54. Pater, *Renaissance*, pp. 221–2.
55. *J* p. 120.
56. Walter Pater, *Marius the Epicurean: His Sensations and Ideas*, New Library edn, London, 1910, repr. 1973, ch. 2, pp. 24–5.
57. Pater, *Renaissance*, p. 221.
58. Pater, *Marius*, ch. 9, p. 146.
59. *J* pp. 120–1.
60. Pater, 'Coleridge's Writings', p. 433.
61. Pater, *Renaissance*, p. 196.
62. Pater, *Renaissance*, p. 129.
63. *J* p. 126, 9 February 1868.
64. Pater, *Renaissance*, p. 217.
65. *J* p. 163, 6 April 1868.
66. *J* p. 259, 10 September 1874.
67. *J* p. 230, 24 February 1874.
68. *FL* p. 202, 10 July 1863.
69. *J* p. 209, 11 May 1871.
70. *J* p. 171, 10 July 1868.
71. *J* p. 200, 20 October 1870.
72. *J* p. 205, March–April 1871.
73. Pater, *Renaissance*, p. 109.
74. Edward Thomas, *Walter Pater: A Critical Study*, London, 1913, p. 96. Thomas' book is dismissed by Ruth Child (*The Aesthetic of Walter Pater*, Darby, Pa., 1969, p. 3) as 'obviously superficial', but his criticism seems to me to hold.
75. Pater, *Renaissance*, p. 123.
76. *Ibid.* p. 134.
77. *Ibid.* p. 128.
78. *Ibid.* p. 205.
79. *Ibid.* p. 218.
80. *Ibid.* p. 218.
81. *Ibid.* p. 219.
82. *J* p. 127.
83. *J* pp. 125–6.
84. *J* p. 248, 12 June 1874.
85. *J* p. 289.
86. *RB* p. 66, 15 February 1879.
87. *C* p. 135, 30 June 1886.
88. Downes, *op. cit.* p. 28.
89. *J* p. 245 (1874).
90. *J* p. 243, 20 April 1874.

91. *J* p. 218, 23 February 1872.
92. *J* p. 174, 16 July 1868.
93. *J* p. 199 (1870).
94. *J* p. 221.
95. *J* p. 254, 17 August 1874.
96. *FL* p. 349, 3 January 1884.
97. Letter to Benjamin Bailey, 22 November 1817, *Letters of John Keats*, ed. Robert Gittings, London, 1970, p. 37.
98. *J* p. 127, 9 February 1868.
99. Efrem Bettoni, *Duns Scotus: The Basic Principles of His Philosophy*, trans. and ed. Bernardine Bonansea, Washington, D. C., 1961, pp. 160–5. On the moral implications of Scotus' voluntarism see also F. C. Copleston, *A History of Medieval Philosophy*, London, 1972, pp. 227–9.
100. Christopher Devlin, *The Psychology of Duns Scotus* (Aquinas Paper 15), Oxford, 1950, p. 15. In my view this is a more valuable piece than Father Devlin's two-part article specifically concerned with the relation between Scotus and Hopkins, 'The Image and the Word', *The Month*, n.s. III (1950), pp. 114–27, 191–202 (cf. also ensuing correspondence). Other works on, or relating to, Scotus which are helpful are: F. C. Copleston, *A History of Philosophy*, London, 1946–75, vol. II, 1950, repr. 1966, pp. 476–551; C. R. S. Harris, *Duns Scotus*, 2 vols., Oxford, 1927; and Sebastian J. Day, *Intuitive Cognition: A Key to the Significance of the Later Scholastics*, New York, 1947, especially pp. 39–139.
101. *S* p. 238.
102. *RB* p. 83, 26 May 1879.
103. There is a difficulty about making the explicit identification when it is not done for us in the poem, and this is that the name tends to act as a focus which makes us look externally at the mythical creature instead of being caught up in the change from potential to actual movement which it exists in the poem to figure. A further difficulty is that by bringing out what is actually submerged and imprecise in the poem one gives a clearer – and, in this case, less satisfactory – picture of what is going on there. The blur of motion with which the sonnet closes moves the 'hurled', the 'wielded' earth too. But clear, rational analysis might prefer the more conventional separation of elements which, neglecting 'rears' and the accelerating pace of 'bold and bolder', confines the stallion in the still-inert hills and brings in a new image of bird flight to figure simple, if extravagant, high spirits.
104. It is the plough, not the earth ('sillion'), which shines; for a cluster of small reasons. If the sillion shone (as of course, delicately, it can), 'plough down' would be adjectival (i.e. ploughed-down) and hyphenated in accordance with Hopkins' usual practice (cf. e.g. 'dapple-dawn-drawn'), but it is not. Earth is ploughed 'up' or turned 'over', not 'down', but a plough moves 'down' the line of its own furrow. Moreover, a focus on 'sillion' would lose equivalence in thought: falcon, plough, and embers *move* and show their essential nature in activity.
105. Cf. e.g. Empson, *Seven Types of Ambiguity*, 3rd edn, 1956, repr. Harmondsworth, 1961, p. 225: '*Confronted suddenly* with the active physical beauty of the bird' (my italics).

106. *J* p. 221, 7 August 1872.
107. *J* p. 225, 14 August 1872.
108. *J* p. 234, 5 August 1873.
109. *J* p. 252, 14 August 1874.
110. *J* p. 257, 3 September 1874.
111. *FL* p. 146, 15 August 1877.
112. *J* p. 210.
113. *J* p. 223, 10 August 1872.
114. *J* p. 230, 24 February.
115. *J* p. 231, 11 May.
116. *J* pp. 241–2.
117. *J* p. 227, 17 September 1872.
118. *RB* p. 66, 15 February, 1879.
119. *S* p. 176.
120. *S* p. 260.
121. *C* p. 95, 1 December.
122. *RB* p. 66, 15 February 1879.
123. *C* p. 138, 3 July 1886.
124. *S* p. 37, 23 November 1879.
125. *RB* p. 85, 22 June, 1879.

CHAPTER THREE: PURGING THE LANGUAGE

1. Letter dated 5 November 1885, sent by Hopkins from Clongowes Wood College, Naas, Ireland, to his brother Everard; published by Anthony Bischoff in *The Times Literary Supplement*, 8 December 1972, p. 1511.
2. *J* p. 23, 14 April 1864.
3. *FL* p. 353n, 2 May 1884, extract from letter of Coventry Patmore to Bridges.
4. *RB* p. 56, 16 July 1878.
5. *C* p. 42, 22 December 1881.
6. *RB* p. 221, 1 September 1885.
7. *RB* p. 297, 19 October 1888.
8. *RB* p. 270, 12 January 1888.
9. *RB* p. 73, 22 February 1879.
10. *RB* p. 219, 17 May 1885.
11. *RB* p. 66, 15 February 1879.
12. *RB* p. 136, 16 September 1881.
13. *FL* p. 379, 12 May 1887.
14. *RB* p. 136, 16 September 1881.
15. See, e.g., *C* p. 42, 22 December 1880, and *RB* p. 48, 2 April 1878.
16. F. R. Leavis, *Gerard Manley Hopkins: Reflections after Fifty Years*, The Hopkins Society Second Annual Lecture, London, 1971, p. 5.
17. *FL* p. 359, 4 April 1885.
18. *FL* p. 336, 23 November 1883.
19. *RB* p. 266, 6 November 1887.
20. *RB* p. 66, 15 February 1879.
21. *RB* p. 89, 14 August 1879; *FL* p. 296, 16 August 1883, to Patmore.
22. *FL* p. 370, 6 October 1886.

23. *RB* p. 39, 3 April 1877.
24. *RB* p. 72, 22 February 1879.
25. *RB* p. 79, 22 April 1879.
26. *RB* p. 73, 22 February 1879.
27. *RB* p. 96, 22 October 1879.
28. *C* p. 8, 13 June 1878.
29. *RB* p. 256, 30 July 1887.
30. *RB* p. 267, 6 November 1887.
31. *RB* p. 277, 25 May 1888.
32. *RB* p. 284, 7 September 1888.
33. *RB* p. 248, 2 January 1887.
34. *FL* p. 370, 6 October 1886.
35. *FL* p. 373, 7 November 1886.
36. *J* p. 289, 'Poetry and Verse'.
37. *RB* p. 130, 14 May 1881.
38. *RB* p. 66, 15 February 1879.
39. *RB* p. 250, 17 February 1887.
40. *RB* p. 293, 3 October 1888.
41. *RB* p. 291, 25 September 1888.
42. F. R. Leavis, *The Common Pursuit*, London, 1952, repr. Harmondsworth, 1962, p. 46.
43. *Poems*, p. 274.
44. W. B. Yeats, Introduction, *The Oxford Book of Modern Verse*, Oxford, 1936, p. xxxix.
45. *RB* p. 83, 26 May 1879.
46. *RB* p. 171, 4 January 1883.
47. N. H. MacKenzie, *Hopkins*, London, 1968, pp. 119–20.
48. *C* p. 153, 22 December 1887.
49. Donald Davie, 'Hopkins as a Decadent Critic', *Purity of Diction in English Verse*, London, 1952, pp. 160–82 (p. 175).
50. *Ibid.*
51. *FL* pp. 381–2, 20 October 1887, to Patmore.
52. *FL* p. 386, 6 May 1888.
53. Leavis, *Common Pursuit*, p. 45.
54. Leavis, *Gerard Manley Hopkins*, p. 6.
55. *J* pp. 267, 'Lecture Notes: Rhetoric'; 289, 'Poetry and Verse'.
56. *RB* pp. 267–8, 6 November 1887.
57. *RB* p. 284, 7 September 1888.
58. *RB* p. 89, 14 August 1879.
59. *J* p. 112.
60. *RB* pp. 267–8, 6 November 1887.
61. Matthew Arnold, *Essays in Criticism*, 2nd series, ed. S. R. Littlewood, London, 1960, p. 25.
62. *RB* p. 280, 18 August 1888.
63. Arnold, *Essays*, p. 2.
64. *Ibid.* p. 23.
65. *Ibid.* p. 23.
66. *Ibid.* p. 47.

67. *Ibid.* p. 47.
68. Repr., *The Poems of Matthew Arnold*, ed. C. B. Tinker and H. F. Lowry, London, 1961, p. xxviii.
69. *C* p. 13, 5 October 1878.
70. *The Times Literary Supplement*, 8 December 1972, p. 1511.
71. Cf., e. g., Marshall McLuhan, *The Gutenberg Galaxy*, London, 1962, p. 238, on this theme.
72. *RB* pp. 51–2, 21 May 1878.
73. *RB* p. 79, 22 April 1879.
74. *RB* p. 157, 18 October 1882.
75. *RB* p. 246, 11 December 1886.
76. *RB* p. 265, November 1887.
77. Cf. *RB* p. 171, 4 January 1883.
78. *RB* p. 273, 10 February 1888.
79. *RB* p. 46, 21 August 1877.
80. *C* p. 14, 5 October 1878.
81. *C* p. 23, 27 February 1879.
82. *C* p. 14, 6 October 1878.
83. *RB* p. 24, 7 August 1868.
84. *J* p. 278, 'Lecture Notes: Rhetoric'.
85. *RB* p. 45, 21 August 1877.
86. *RB* p. 156, 18 October 1882.
87. W. K. Wimsatt, *Hateful Contraries*, Lexington, Ky., 1965, p. 130.
88. *Ibid.* pp. 142–3.
89. *Ibid.* p. 145.
90. *RB* p. 45, 21 August 1877.
91. *C* pp. 40–1, 22 December 1880.
92. *FL* p. 327, 7 November 1883.
93. Reproduced in facsimile, *RB* facing p. 262.
94. *RB* p. 81, 26 May 1879.
95. *C* p. 39, 22 December 1880.
96. *C* p. 41, 22 December 1880.
97. *Poems*, pp. 47–8.
98. *RB* p. 157, 18 October 1882.
99. *RB* p. 303, 21 March 1889.
100. *RB* p. 246, 11 December 1886.
101. *RB* p. 245, 26 November 1886.
102. *C* pp. 41–2, 22 December 1880.
103. See *J* p. 382, n163:3.
104. *The Dragon in the Gate: Studies in the Poetry of Gerard Manley Hopkins*, Berkeley and Los Angeles, 1968, p. 89.
105. *Ibid.* p. 87.
106. *RB* p. 122, 26 January 1881.
107. *C* p. 87, 29 October 1881.
108. Yeats, Introduction, *Oxford Book of Modern Verse*, p. xl.
109. *J* p. 102, 'On the Origin of Beauty'.
110. *FL* p. 124, 29 August 1874.
111. *FL* p. 126, 1 September 1874, to his mother.

112. *J* p. 258, 6 September 1874.
113. See *RB* p. 31, 20 February 1875: 'I have tried to learn a little Welsh, in reality one of the hardest of languages'; *FL* p. 142, 23 September 1876, to his mother, in which he refers to 'the good woman who did teach me Welsh'; and *FL* p. 146, 20 April 1877, to his mother, about a visit to Caernarvon: 'It was for my Welsh that I went.'
114. *FL* p. 140, 6 August 1876, to his father.
115. *FL* p. 241, 6 January 1877.
116. *C* p. 15, 5 October 1878.
117. *RB* p. 163, 26 November 1882.
118. H. I. Bell, *The Development of Welsh Poetry*, Oxford, 1936, p. 42.
119. Hopkins' adopted bardic signature. See *Poems* pp. 254, 326.
120. Gweneth Lilly, 'The Welsh Influence in the Poetry of Gerard Manley Hopkins', *Modern Language Review*, XXXVIII (1943), pp. 192–205.
121. It is worth indicating that Hopkins' first recorded interest in Welsh was a very early one – he copied a Welsh verse in 1864 – but this hardly detracts from Miss Lilly's conclusions, which are based on the fact that his first systematic study of the language was at St Beuno's. See *J* p. 34 (1864) and p. 316, n34:2.
122. *RB* p. 163, 26 November 1882.
123. Lilly, *op. cit.* p. 196.
124. *Ibid.* p. 203.
125. *RB* p. 217, 17 May 1885.
126. *RB* p. 159, 21 October 1882.

CHAPTER FOUR: ETERNAL MAY-TIME

1. *St. Winefred's Well*, *Poems* p. 193.
2. 'The Wreck of the Deutschland', stanza 24.
3. *FL* p. 370, 6 October 1886, to Coventry Patmore.
4. *RB* p. 227, 2 October 1886.
5. *RB* p. 228, 2 October 1886.
6. Cf., e.g., T. S. Eliot, *After Strange Gods*, London, 1934, p. 48.
7. F. R. Leavis, *The Common Pursuit*, London, 1952, repr. Harmondsworth, 1962, p. 50.
8. *J* p. 230, 17 April 1873.
9. *FL* p. 145, 3 March 1877.
10. *RB* p. 218, 17 May 1885.
11. *FL* p. 111, 1 March 1870.
12. *RB* p. 28, 2 August 1871.
13. *C* p. 97, 1 December 1881.
14. *RB* pp. 127–8, 1 May 1881.
15. *FL* p. 293, 1 May 1888, to A. W. M. Baillie. In what seems a flat contradiction of the account I give, Hopkins had written *before* he worked in the cities of the north, 'Horrible to say, in a manner I am a Communist. Their ideal bating some things is nobler than that professed by any secular statesman I know of (I must own I live in bat-light and shoot at a venture). Besides it is just. – I do not mean the means of getting to it are. But it is a dreadful thing

for the greatest and most necessary part of a very rich nation to live a hard life without dignity, knowledge, comforts, delight, or hopes in the midst of plenty – which plenty they make' (*RB* pp. 27–8, 2 August 1871). In fact, Hopkins' politics became increasingly conservative as he grew older, but the point I would make about this passage is that the capacity for human sympathy evident in this analysis-at-a-distance was seriously interfered with when he had immediate personal experience of urban wretchedness: the ugliness of squalor overcame him.

16. *J* p. 130, 9 February 1868.
17. MS C.ii at Campion Hall, Oxford. Anthony Bischoff does not agree with the view given above. He says (in 'The Manuscripts of Hopkins', *Thought*, XXVI (1951-2), p. 567, referring to the same diary confession-notes, but under a different reference system), '*Quoted out of context* such passages might indicate that at this time Hopkins was homosexual; in context, however, they prove quite the contrary.' It seems to me that the context does not alter the fact that they show homosexual feeling.
18. *RB* p. 61, 19 January 1879.
19. *S* pp. 34–8, a sermon for 23 November 1879.
20. *RB* p. 131, 16 June 1881.
21. *J* p. 261, 8 October 1874.
22. *J* p. 236, 16 August 1873.

CHAPTER FIVE: THE CAVERNOUS DARK

1. Walter Pater, *The Renaissance: Studies in Art and Poetry*, with an introduction by Kenneth Clark, London, 1961, p. 223.
2. *S* p. 90, 25 October 1880.
3. *The Times*, Monday 13 December 1875, p. 9, col. 4, reprinted in *Immortal Diamond: Studies in Gerard Manley Hopkins*, ed. Norman Weyand, London, 1949, p. 369.
4. *Ibid.* p. 372.
5. *RB* p. 208, 24 March 1885.
6. *S* p. 169. Hopkins shared in the excitement generated by the Victorian 'golden age' of mountaineering. In 1868, immediately before joining the Jesuits, he had been on holiday in Switzerland (see *J* pp. 168–84), where he had climbed the Breithorn and met the scientist John Tyndall preparing to climb the Matterhorn. The first ascent of this last peak, then regarded as a major challenge, had been made only three years before Hopkins' holiday by Edward Whymper, and the second incident referred to in Hopkins' meditation-note above is, in fact, a description of the accident which befell Whymper's party on the descent, except that the 'four' who went headlong were killed when the rope linking them to the rest of the party broke. Hopkins wrote of the Alps, 'How fond of and warped to the mountains it would be easy to become! For every cliff and limb and edge and jutty has its own nobility.' (*J* p. 172, 11 July 1868). Apart from his references to the securing rope, his alpine interest perhaps shows again in the 'mountains, cliffs of fall' of 'No worst, there is none'.
7. J. E. Keating, '*The Wreck of the Deutschland*': *An Essay and Commentary*,

Kent State University Bulletin (Research Series 6), 1963, p. 55. See Job 10:8, 'Thine hands have made me and fashioned me together round about; yet thou dost destroy me', and 10:11, 'Thou hast clothed me with skin and flesh, and hast fenced me with bones and sinews.'

8. Elizabeth Schneider, *The Dragon in the Gate: Studies in the Poetry of Gerard Manley Hopkins*, Berkeley and Los Angeles, 1968, pp. 26–33; *RB* p. 50, 21 May 1878.

9. *S* p. 200, 8 November 1881.

10. F. R. Leavis, *The Common Pursuit*, London, 1952, repr. Harmondsworth, 1962, p. 57.

11. Pater, *Renaissance*, p. 224.

12. Pater, *Renaissance*, p. 196.

13. Editorial note by Bridges repr. in *Poems*, p. 296.

14. *Ibid.*

CHAPTER SIX: IRELAND

1. *S* p. 262, Retreat-notes for 2 January 1889 (not 1888; see *FL* p. 190, n. 3).

2. W. H. Gardner, *Gerard Manley Hopkins 1844–1889: A Study of Poetic Idiosyncrasy in relation to Poetic Tradition*, 2 vols., London, 1958, vol. I, p. 180.

3. David A. Downes, *Gerard Manley Hopkins: A Study of His Ignatian Spirit*, New York, 1959, pp. 135–6.

4. *S* p. 263, 5 January 1889.

5. *FL* p. 63, 20 February 1884.

6. *RB* p. 190, 7 March 1884.

7. *RB* p. 190.

8. *RB* p. 193, 30 April 1884.

9. *C* p. 122, 9 July 1884.

10. *RB* p. 195, 3 August 1884.

11. *C* p. 123, 25 October 1884.

12. *FL* p. 163, 26 November 1884, to his mother.

13. *RB* p. 201, 1 January 1885.

14. *RB* pp. 214–15, 1 April 1885.

15. Cf. *FL* p. 256, 17 May 1885, to A. W. M. Baillie, and *RB* p. 216, 17 May 1885.

16. *RB* p. 222, 1 September 1885.

17. *RB* pp. 226–9, 2 October. He also visited Bridges in May that year (*RB* pp. 224–5, 4 May).

18. *RB* pp. 258–9, 25 August 1887.

19. *RB* pp. 278–9, 282, 284–5 18 August, 7 September, and 10 September 1888).

20. *RB* p. 282, 7 September 1888.

21. *RB* p. 250, 17 February 1887.

22. *FL* pp. 184–5, 5 July 1888. Contrast his view of his work in Liverpool: 'There is merit in it but little Muse' (*C* p. 33, 14 May 1880).

23. *FL* p. 163, 26 November 1884, to his mother.

24. *FL* p. 173, 13 November 1885, to his mother.

25. *S* p. 261, Retreat-notes, 1 January 1889.

26. *RB* p. 126, 27 April 1881.
27. *RB* p. 135, 16 September 1881.
28. *FL* p. 142, 23 September 1876.
29. *RB* p. 55, 13 July 1878.
30. *FL* p. 245, 9 June 1880, to Baillie.
31. *RB* p. 190, 7 March 1884.
32. *RB* p. 216, 17 May 1885.
33. *FL* p. 292, 1 May 1888, to Baillie.
34. *FL* p. 293, *ibid.* (Hopkins' ellipsis.)
35. *RB* p. 136, 16 September 1881.
36. *C* p. 42, 22 December 1880.
37. *RB* p. 48, 2 April 1878.
38. *RB* p. 221, 1 September 1885.
39. *A Page of Irish History: Story of University College, Dublin, 1883–1909*, compiled by Fathers of the Society of Jesus, 1930, p. 104, repr. *RB* p. 319 as n. v.
40. *Poems*, Introduction, p. xlii.
41. Michael Black, 'The Musical Analogy', *English*, xxv, Summer 1976, pp. 111–34 (p. 121).
42. *FL* p. 276, 20 February 1887, to Baillie.
43. Cf. Genesis 32:24–30.
44. *RB* p. 221, 1 September 1885.
45. Yvor Winters, in *The Function of Criticism*, Denver, 1957, repr. in *Hopkins: A Collection of Critical Essays*, ed. Geoffrey H. Hartman, Englewood Cliffs, 1966, pp. 45–6.
46. Cf. John 14:26.
47. N. H. MacKenzie, *Hopkins*, London, 1968, p. 93.
48. *King Lear* IV. i. 27–8.
49. *Macbeth* II. ii. 37.
50. For an opposed view see G. F. Lahey, *Gerard Manley Hopkins*, London, 1930, pp. 139–40: 'his work itself was interesting and consoling, and his friends congenial and satisfying; then too, the monotony of routine was easily broken by the utmost freedom he had received from his superiors. It is necessary to insist on this because so many writers have drawn tragic portraits of an exiled Englishman slowly dying of loneliness, drudgery, and despair.' It is no criticism of either Hopkins' friends or his superiors to note that the evidence of both his prose and his verse is against Lahey in this.
51. *FL* p. 256, 8 May 1885.
52. *RB* p. 216, 17 May 1885.
53. *RB* p. 222, 1 September 1885.
54. *S* pp. 261–2.
55. *RB* p. 257, 30 July 1887.
56. *RB* p. 300, 23 February 1889.
57. *RB* p. 210, 24 March 1885.
58. Cf. Matthew 10:34–7.
59. *S* p. 146.
60. *S* p. 118.
61. *S* p. 123, 20 August 1880.

62. Though the reference in this case is before Hopkins' time in Ireland, cf., e.g., 'Dearest Bridges, – I wish you would write; it makes me disconsolate punctually every morning to get no letter.' (*RB* p. 178, 19 April 1883.)
63. *FL* p. 255, 24 April 1885.
64. *FL* pp. 213–14, 20 July and 14 August 1864.
65. F. R. Leavis, *Gerard Manley Hopkins: Reflections after Fifty Years*, The Hopkins Society Second Annual Lecture, London, 1971, p. 15.
66. *S* p. 262, Retreat-notes, 1 January 1889.
67. The 'shame ... when with men I deal' is not adequately accounted for in the poem by the futility of the Alchemist's endeavours: it may be that we have here an oblique reference to Hopkins' homosexual feelings, though there is no other warranty in the poem for supposing this.
68. *RB* p. 270, 12 January 1888.
69. *C* pp. 108–9, 25 June 1883.
70. *FL* pp. 275–6, 20 February 1887, to Baillie.
71. *FL* p. 368, 4 June 1886.
72. *RB* p. 231, 13 October 1886.
73. Matthew 19:12.
74. *RB* p. 270, 12 January 1888: 'Nothing comes: I am a eunuch – but it is for the kingdom of heaven's sake.'
75. *RB* p. 222, 1 September 1885, and *S* p. 262, 1 January 1889.
76. *FL* p. 197, 5 May 1889.

INDEX